Patrick Weston Joyce, John William Glover

Ancient Irish Music

Patrick Weston Joyce, John William Glover

Ancient Irish Music

ISBN/EAN: 9783742814548

Manufactured in Europe, USA, Canada, Australia, Japa

Cover: Foto ©Angelika Wolter / pixelio.de

Manufactured and distributed by brebook publishing software (www.brebook.com)

Patrick Weston Joyce, John William Glover

Ancient Irish Music

ANCIENT IRISH MUSIC:

COMPRISING

ONE HUNDRED AIRS HITHERTO UNPUBLISHED,
MANY OF THE OLD POPULAR SONGS,
AND SEVERAL NEW SONGS.

Collected and Edited
BY
P. W. JOYCE, LL.D., M.R.I.A.

The Harmonies
By PROFESSOR GLOVER.

" —— some notes we used to love
In days of boyhood ——."

DUBLIN:
McGLASHAN AND GILL, UPPER SACKVILLE-STREET.
LONDON: SIMPKIN, MARSHALL, & CO.   EDINBURGH: JOHN MENZIES & CO.
1873.

PREFACE.

IN the year 1855 was published "The Ancient Music of Ireland," a volume which was edited by George Petrie, LL.D., under the superintendence of the "Society for the preservation and publication of the Melodies of Ireland." This volume contains a large number of airs, of which about twenty were contributed by me. It was my wish that all my collection, or all worthy of preservation, should be printed by the Society, but the publication ceased after the appearance of one volume. The death of Dr. Petrie, in 1864, put an end to all hope of continuing the work; for he left no one behind him who was, at that time at least, either able or willing to undertake the editorship. His death was indeed an irreparable loss: for he possessed an extensive and critical knowledge of the subject, which it is to be feared few or none will ever equal. My only anxiety was to secure the publication of the airs I had preserved, that they might be saved from possible loss; but as I failed to do so under the auspices of the Society, I am now doing what I suppose is the next best thing, publishing them myself.

I spent all my early life in a part of the country where music and dancing were favourite amusements; and as I loved the graceful music of the people from my childhood, their songs, dance tunes, *keens*, and lullabies remained on my memory, almost without any effort of my own. I had indeed excellent opportunities; for my father's memory was richly stored with popular airs and songs; and I believe he never sang or played a tune that I did not learn. Afterwards, when I came to reside in Dublin, and became acquainted with the various published collections of Irish music, I was surprised to find that a great number of my tunes were unpublished, and quite unknown outside the district or province in which they had been learned. This discovery stimulated me to write down all the airs I could recollect; and when my own memory was exhausted, I went among the peasantry during vacations, for several successive years, noting down whatever I thought worthy of preserving, both music and words. In this way I gradually accumulated a very large collection.

There yet remains a great quantity of music among the people, unpublished and uncollected. But it is fast dying out; and those who are gifted with sufficient musical knowledge and taste should catch and write down the fugitive strains before they are extinguished for ever. If the old harpers had not been brought together in Belfast in 1792, by the patriotic exertions of Dr. Macdonnell and a few other gentlemen, Bunting probably would never have entered on the task of preserving his country's music, and the greater number of tunes in his noble collection would have been lost to us; for in a very few years after, the harpers were all dead and gone. And now, if those among us who understand and love Irish music, exert ourselves even in a small way, like those Belfast gentlemen, we shall, like them, have some claims on the gratitude of posterity. For me, I shall be thankful to any person who sends me one or more Irish airs or songs; for I will continue to publish as long as I can obtain materials; provided such matter as the present little volume contains, meet with the approval of the public.

In modern music the seventh note of the minor scale is generally raised half a tone, so as to bring it within a semitone of the octave. This, however, was hardly ever done in Irish airs in the minor mode; and an illustration of this remark will be found in almost every minor air in the present collection. I cannot help observing that editors of Irish music appear to me to be often too much inclined to force those of the Irish airs that are in the minor scale into a compliance with the modern rule, thereby, in many instances, falsifying the airs, and depriving them of their antique character.

I had intended to offer a few observations on the subject of harmony; and in particular I was anxious to record the opinion that the accompaniments ought to be extremely simple;—that in fact abstruse or complicated harmonies commonly destroy the character of Irish melodies. But Professor Glover has favoured me with a letter in which these views are put forward in language so precise and instructive, as to render quite unnecessary any further observations of mine.

" 14, Talbot Street, Dublin, November 19th, 1872.

" DEAR DR. JOYCE,

"As you have confided to me the task of clothing your Irish tunes in suitable harmonies, I think it necessary to mention that simple as the task may seem, it required some discrimination. Some of the tunes are regular, and subject to the rules of counterpoint; others are wild and desultory, and such as do not readily admit the accompaniment of a bass: while many again are of a mixed kind, partaking of both these characteristics. In giving them suitable harmonies, I have been guided by the obvious principle of not attempting a harmony when doing so would injure the character of the tune, as in case of the *Keens* and Lullabies. In tunes partaking of the mixed character, I have found it expedient to vary the treatment, so as to be in keeping with the melody; for in many tunes of this class the point and interest lies in a few notes occasionally at the end of each part. In such tunes, by alternating a simple harmony with a bit of vigorous unison—so that the point of the melody will be readily understood—the character of the music is more distinctively preserved. I have avoided all abstruse treatment as out of place; and I have merely endeavoured to give the melodies such natural harmonies as will be in accordance with their character, and at the same time will enable them to be readily caught up by the popular ear, and to be retained there.

Yours faithfully, J. W. GLOVER."

I think I am bound to mention that Professor Glover not only harmonised the airs, but assisted me throughout: I had, in fact, all the advantage that could be derived from the presence and advice of an accomplished scientific musician.

The Dance tunes that prevailed in the Munster counties, twenty-five or thirty years ago, were chiefly the Reel, the Double Jig, the Single Jig, the Hop Jig, and the Hornpipe. The Reel was in common, or two-four time. The Double Jig was a six-eight time tune, the bars of which usually consisted of six quavers in two triplets. The Single Jig was also six-eight time; but here the triplet of the Double Jig was generally, though not invariably, represented by a crotchet followed by a quaver. The Hop Jig, or as it was also called, Slip Jig, or Slip Time, was a nine-eight time tune. The Hornpipe was in common, or two-four time; it was played not quite so quickly as the Reel, and was always danced by a man unaccompanied by a partner. All these dance tunes, except the last, took their names from the manner in which they were danced. Besides these, there were "Set Dance" tunes, *i.e.* tunes with some peculiarity of time, measure, or length, which required a special sort of dance, that had to be learned and practised for each particular tune. A Set Dance was always danced by a man without a partner. On the subject of the Munster dances I may take advantage of some other opportunity to make a few observations.

The time in which each tune is to be played is indicated by the swing of a simple pendulum. Hang a little weight—a heavy button, a bullet, &c—to the end of a thread, and after measuring it to the length indicated at the head of the tune, suspend it from the finger, or from a nail, and set it swinging; it will show at once the time in which the tune is to be played. For instance, in the first tune, page 2, let the thread from the finger to the weight be 20 inches, then each swing will indicate the length of a crotchet. The time I have indicated for the dance tunes is not quite so fast as they were played for dancing.

In connection with the subject of time or movement, I will venture an opinion that our song tunes are generally played and sung too slowly: while on the other hand, the dance music is often played too fast; and in both cases the sentiment of the air is injured —sometimes utterly destroyed. To understand and appreciate a song tune, the ear of the listener must, as it were, catch the pace of the melody; which is extremely difficult when it is played too slowly, and still more so if it be overloaded with harmony. And in this manner a tune, exquisitely beautiful when understood, may be made to a listener—even though he be a skilled musician—quite unintelligible, and devoid of all sentiment. On this subject, Bunting makes the following interesting observations:—" When the meeting of the harpers took place at Belfast, in 1792, the editor, being selected to note down the tunes, was surprised to find that all the melodies played by the harpers were performed with a much greater degree of quickness than he had till then been accustomed to. The harpers made those airs assume quite a new character, spirited, lively, and energetic, certainly according much more with the national disposition, than the languid and tedious manner in which they were, and too often still are, played among fashionable public performers, in whose efforts at realizing a false conception of sentiment, the melody is very often so attenuated as to be all but lost." (Ancient Music of Ireland; page 18.)

I now offer to the public a part of my collection of Airs and Songs; and if each of my readers derive from them even a tithe of the exquisite enjoyment they have afforded me during the greater part of my life, then it may be truly said that they are well worth publication.

P. W. JOYCE.

Dublin, December 1872.

CONTENTS.

NUMBER.	NAME.	PAGE.
1.	The Fairy King's Courtship	1
2.	The Barley Grain	3
3.	Slán Beó. Farewell	4
4.	An Súiste Buidhe. The Yellow Flail.	5
5.	An Súiste Buidhe. The Yellow Flail. (2nd. air)	6
6.	The Flannel Jacket. Reel.	6
7.	Hop Jig	7
8.	Fáinne geal an lae. The Dawning of the day.	8
9.	Ban-lanna. The Ale woman	10
10.	Crabs in the skillet	11
11.	Och-ochone	11
12.	Maidin cheódhach nuair d'cirigheas. When I rose on a misty morning	12
13.	Fagamaoid súd mar ata sé. Let us leave that as it is	13
14.	Aon is dó na piobaireachta. The Ace and Deuce of Pipering	14
15.	'Tis not your gold would me entice	16
16.	Reel	17
17.	I'm going to be married on Sunday	17
18.	The Summer is come and the grass is green	19
19.	Kennedy's Jig	20
20.	The Mountains high	21
21.	An Cumhain leatsa an oidhche úd? Do you remember that night?	22
22.	Ceapach Dáinig. Cappadanig	24
23.	The Green Bushes	25
24.	Air	26
25.	We are the boys of Wexford	27
26.	Cheer up, cheer up, daughter	27
27.	Lamentation air	29
28.	Na mná deasa an Bhaile-Locha-Riabhach. The pretty lasses of Loughrea	30
29.	Spéir-bhean. The Bright Lady	31
30.	The Shanavest and Caravat. A faction tune	32
31.	Single Jig	33
32.	Bealltaine. May day	34
33.	Slán agus Beannacht le buairidhibh a'tsaoghail. Farewell to the troubles of the world	35

CONTENTS.

NUMBER.	NAME.	PAGE.
34.	*Astoreen Machree.* O treasure of my heart	36
35.	How do you like her for your wife?	37
36.	*Faghaim arís a' cruiscín as biodh se lán.* We'll take again a cruiskeen, a cruiskeen laun	38
37.	The Job of Journeywork. A set dance	38
38.	*Draharéen-O-Machree.* Little brother of my heart	39
39.	The lovely sweet banks of the Suir	41
40.	*An ceó Draoigheachta.* The Magic Mist	42
41.	Jig	43
42.	The Shamrock Shore	44
43.	The wee wee bag of *praties*	45
44.	There was a bold beggarman	45
45.	Alas, my little bag	46
46.	*Be n-Eirinn I.* Whoe'er she be	47
47.	*Mór Chluana.* More of Cloyne	48
48.	The top of Cork Road	48
49.	Roving Jack of all trades	49
50.	Reynard the Fox. A hunting song	50
51.	Reel	51
52.	*Cumail a' mháilín.* Rub the bag	52
53.	*Fead an iolair.* The Eagle's whistle	53
54.	*An Ciarraigheacht malluightha.* The wicked Kerryman	54
55.	Cold and rough the north wind blows	55
56.	*An tiocfadh tu a bhaile liom?* Will you come home with me?	57
57.	*Thaunalaw.* It is day	57
58.	King Charles's Jig	59
59.	*Caoine. A Keen or Lament.*	59
60.	Nelly my love and me	60
61.	The Croppy Boy	62
62.	Reel	63
63.	Along with my love I'll go	63
64.	In comes great Bonaparte	65
65.	*Bata na bplandaighe.* The Planting stick	66
66.	*Suantraidhe* (Soontree). Lullaby	67
67.	Fair Maidens' beauty will soon fade away	68
68.	The Lowlands of Holland	69
69.	The Funny Tailor	70
70.	Round the world for sport. Jig.	71
71.	*An Cnuicín fraoigh.* The Knockeen-free (Heathy little hill)	72
72.	I'm a poor stranger and far from my own	73
73.	*Suantraidhe* (Soontree). Lullaby	74
74.	Come all you maids where'er you be	75
75.	Captain Thompson	76
76.	*Suantraidhe* (Soontree). Lullaby	77
77.	The Gorey Caravan	78

CONTENTS.

NUMBER	NAME	PAGE
78.	Barbara Allen	79
79.	Young Roger was a ploughboy	80
80.	The field of hay. Jig	82
81.	No Surrender	82
82.	Tea in the morning. Hop Jig	84
83.	It is to fair England I'm willing to go	85
84.	The game played in Erin-go-bragh	85
85.	The blooming Meadows. Jig.	87
86.	Billy Byrne of Ballymanus	88
87.	The little horse tied at a Public-house	89
88.	*Suantraidhe.* Lullaby	90
89.	There was an old astrologer	91
90.	Pretty Peggy	92
91.	The boys of the Town. Jig	93
92.	Bessie	94
93.	Adieu, lovely Mary	94
94.	Strop the Razor. Jig.	96
95.	Billy the barber shaved his father	97
96.	Dobbin's flowery vale	98
97.	Una	99
98.	The Leprehaun	100
99.	*Mo ghradh bán a'm threigan.* My fair love leaving me	102
100.	The Lake of Coolfin, or Willy Leonard	103

ANCIENT IRISH MUSIC.

No. 1.

BOTH the air and the words of this ballad appear to me to possess much simple beauty and feeling. I learned them from my father when I was a mere child, and I never heard the air with any one else. The words are still sung in some parts of Munster, though so very much corrupted as to be quite barbarous; but I do not know whether they retain the air. I have amended several corrupt stanzas.

This ballad embodies one of the many forms of a superstition formerly very prevalent in Ireland, and not quite extinct even at the present day—namely, a belief that the fairies often take away mortals to their palaces in the fairy forts, *lisses*, and pleasant green hills. Macananty or Macanantan was a fairy chief or king who formerly enjoyed great celebrity in the north of Ireland, and whose fame extended also into the south. There is a hill called Scraba in the county of Down, about eight miles from Belfast, near the top of which is a great sepulchral cairn. Under this hill and cairn Macananty had his palace; and the place still retains much of its fairy reputation among the peasantry of the district.

Macananty himself is remembered in legend, and his name is quite familiar, especially among the people who inhabit the mountainous districts extending from Dundalk to Newcastle in the county of Down. I find that here they call him in Irish *Sheamus Macaneandan*—James Macanantan; but both names, John and James, must have been added in recent times. He is mentioned in one of Neilson's Irish dialogues in the following words:—
"They set out at cock-crowing, from smooth Knock-Magha forth, both Finvar and his valiant host. And many a fairy castle, rath, and mount, they shortly visited, from dawn of day till fall of night, on beautiful winged coursers. * * * * They never halted; for they were to sup that Hallow-eve in the fairy castle of Scraba, with the fairy chief Macaneantan."—(Neilson's Irish Gram. pp. 57, 58, 59.) I have not found him mentioned however in any ancient Irish authority.

Notwithstanding the northern origin of the fairy chief, it is probable that both air and words are of Munster origin. This appears clear enough, both from the fact that the song prevails in Munster, and from the internal evidence afforded by several of the stanzas. It would appear that Macananty must have seen, in some preternatural way, a vision of the

B

maiden before meeting with her; that after travelling "by sea and by land," he found her in Munster; and that he finally induced her to become his queen.

I suppose the "Queen Anne" of the eighth stanza, is Aine, a fairy princess whom we find frequently mentioned in very ancient Irish writings; she had her palace at the hill of Knockany in the county Limerick, which indeed took its name (Aine's hill) from her; and she was still more celebrated than Macananty. The change of the name Aine to Anne makes me suspect that the ballad is a translation; but although I have searched almost as much as Macananty himself, "I never could find" an Irish original.

1. On the first day of May at the close of the day,
   As I stood in the shade of a green-spreading tree,
   A young lover a-courting a maiden I spied;
   I drew very nigh them to hear and see.

2. The dress that he wore was a velvet so green,
   All trimmed with gold lace, and as bright as the sea;
   And he said, "Love, I'll make you my own fairy queen,
   "If you are but willing to go with me.

3. "Lisses and forts shall be at your command,
   "Mountains and valleys, the land and the sea,
   "And the billows that roar along the sea shore,
   "If you are but willing to go with me."

4. "To make me a queen my birth is too mean,
   "And you will get ladies of higher degree;
   "I know not your name nor from whence you came,
   "So I am not willing to go with thee."

5. "I will tell you my name and I love you the same
   "As if you were a lady of higher degree;
   "John Macananty's my name, and from Scraba I came,
   "And the queen of that country my love shall be."

6. "If I were to go with one I don't know,
   "My parents and friends would be angry with me;
   "They would bring me back again with shame and disdain,
   "So I am not willing to go with thee."

7. "From your friends we will sail in a ship that won't fail,
   "With silken top-sail and a wonderful flight;
   "From this to Coleraine, to France and to Spain,
   "And home back again in one short night.

8. "There is not a fort from this to the north
   "But we'll dance around it and sing merrilie;
   "And the lads of queen Anne shall be at your command,
   "And they shall all stand in great dread of thee.

9. "Many a mile I have roamed in my time,
   "By sea and by land a-looking for thee,
   "And I never could find rest or peace for my mind,
   "Until fortune proved kind and sent you to me!"

No. 2.

I took down this tune in 1854 from the whistling of James Quain, a farmer, still living in Coolfree, on the borders of the counties of Cork and Limerick. It belongs to that class of dance tunes called in Munster by the name of "Double jig," a term which will be found explained in the Preface. James Quain stated that it was considered a very old tune, and that it was known to only very few of the people.

4 ANCIENT IRISH MUSIC.

THE BARLEY GRAIN.

Jig time.

No. 3.

This beautiful air I noted down in the year 1853, from the singing of a national schoolmaster, a native of Kerry; and I also took down the words of the Irish song, which I regret I am now unable to find among my papers. Neither can I give the teacher's name, which was written along with the song.

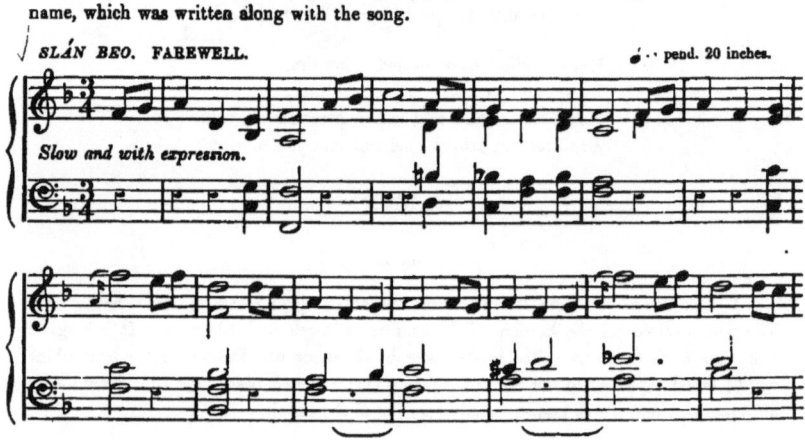

SLÁN BEO. FAREWELL.

Slow and with expression.

No. 4.

This air I have known from my childhood, and always by the name of the "*Súiste buidhe*," or "The yellow flail." But the air immediately following (No. 5), which I noted down from the singing of Joseph Martin, a native of the county Limerick, was, according to him, known by the same name. They are both similar in character and expression—airy and graceful in movement; and as they are precisely alike in measure and rhythm, it is probable that an Irish song called "*Suiste Buidhe*," was sung to both indifferently, and gave them the same name. Observe that both are song airs, and are to be played somewhat slower than double jig time.

AN SÚISTE BUIDHE. THE YELLOW FLAIL.

No. 5.

(See Notice to No. 4).

AN SÚISTE BUIDHE. THE YELLOW FLAIL. (2nd. Air.)

No. 6.

This was a favourite dance tune, twenty-five or thirty years ago in the county Limerick, where I learned it from constantly hearing it played by fiddlers and pipers. I also heard it often called by the name of "The peeler's jacket."

THE FLANNEL JACKET. Reel.

No. 7.

The term "hop-jig," applied in the south of Ireland to dance tunes in nine-eight time, will be found explained in the Preface. I noted this tune from the flute playing of David Grady, a native of Ardpatrick in the county Limerick, but unfortunately I neglected to ascertain its name.

HOP JIG.

8   ANCIENT IRISH MUSIC.

No. 8.

This simple and pleasing melody is a good representative of a very numerous class of Irish airs, all characterized by one peculiarity of structure. There are in reality only two different strains, and the whole tune is made up in the following way:—first strain—second strain—second strain—first strain. In the present air, each strain consists of four bars, and bearing this in mind, the structure will be apparent at a glance.

The Irish song from which the air has taken its name, is still well known in the southern counties. It was published in 1847, with a metrical translation, by Edward Walsh, in his "Irish Popular Songs," an excellent little work, which is now out of print, and difficult to be procured. A rude, though not very incorrect translation used to be sung as a street ballad in my young days. I give the Irish words, accompanied by a translation of my own, the only merit of which is, that it follows the original almost word for word. Lough Lene is the old name of the lakes of Killarney. *Cuilfhionn-deas* (pron. Cooleen-dhas) means pretty fair-haired maiden.

FÁINNE GEAL AN LAE.   THE DAWNING OF THE DAY.

ANCIENT IRISH MUSIC.

1. Maidin mhoch do ghabhas amach
    Air bhruach Locha Léin;
   An samhradh ag teachd, 'san chraobh re n'ais,
    'Gus lonnradh teith ó'n ngréin;
   Air taisdiol dham tre bhailte-puirt
    'Gus bánta míne réidh,
   Cia gheabhainn le'm ais acht cúilfhionn deas
    Le fáinne geal an lae.

2. Ní raibh bróg ná stócaidh, cóip, na clóca,
    Air mo stór ó'n spéir;
   Acht folt fionn órdha sios go troigh
    Ag fás go bárr an fhéir;
   Bhidh calán cruidhte aice 'na glaic,
    'S air driúcht ba dheas a sgéimh;
   Thug barr-ghean ó Venus deas,
    Le fáinne geal an lae.

3. Do shuidh an bhrighdeach síos le 'm ais
    Air bhinnse glas don bhféur;
   A magadh léi bhios dá mhuidheamh go pras
    Mar mhnaoi nach sgarfainn léi;
   A dubhairt sí liom na bris mo chlu,
    Sgaoil mé air siubhal, a reic,
   Sin.iad a ndeas na soillse ag teachd
    Le fáinne geal an lae.

TRANSLATION.

1. One morning early I walked forth
    By the margin of Lough Lene;
   The sunshine dressed the trees in green,
    And summer bloomed again;
   I left the town and wandered on
    Through fields all green and gay;
   And whom should I meet but Coolecn-dhas,
    By the dawning of the day.

2. No cap or cloak this maiden wore,
    Her neck and feet were bare;
   Down to the grass in ringlets fell
    Her glossy golden hair;
   A milking pail was in her hand,
    She was lovely young and gay;
   She bore the palm from Venus bright,
    By the dawning of the day.

3. On a mossy bank I sat me down,
   With the maiden by my side;
   With gentle words I courted her,
   And asked her for my bride;
   She said "Young man, don't bring me blame,
   "But let me go away,
   "For morning's light is shining bright,
   "By the dawning of the day."

No. 9.

I learned this air from the singing of my father. I recollect hearing an Irish song to it, every verse of which ended with the words "Banalanna, banalanna!"

BANALANNA. THE ALE WOMAN.

ANCIENT IRISH MUSIC. 11

No. 10.

Noted down in 1854 from James Buckley, a Limerick piper, who stated his belief that the tune belonged to the county Clare.

No. 11.

I have known this air and heard it sung as long as I can remember. Of the Irish song I give one stanza which it is not necessary to translate; the whole song was a sort of lament (but not a death song), every stanza of which ended with the words "Och-ochone!"

Fóil, fóil a dhuine, no air buile ataoi tu ?
Go de an fáth do chumann agus na faca ariamh thu ?
Is cailín beag óg me do seóladh a'd lionsa ;
Mo bheannacht go buan duit, agus ná déan díth dhom,
Och-ochón !

OCH OCHONE.

No. 12.

I took this air with an Irish song, from the singing of Nora Dwane of Glenosheen in the county Limerick, who still lives in the same neighbourhood. I afterwards found that the song had been published and translated by Edward Walsh, in his Irish Popular Songs ; and I give one stanza with his translation, which, although it is by no means close, will serve to show the rhythm of the song, and its adaptation to the melody.

MAIDIN CHEÓDHACH NUAIR D'EIRIGHEAS. WHEN I ROSE ON A MISTY MORNING.

Maidin cheódhach nuair d'eirigheas,
Is chuadhas amach fa'n gcoill ghlas,
Is ann do bhúail an tréighid me
    Nach leighisfear, faraoir!
Do chuala an bhruinneall mhéidhreach,
A lúib na coille droighneach,
Do phreab mo chroidhe le greann di,
    Gur dhéigh-bhean dam í!

One morn when mists did hover
The green-wood's foliage over,
Twas then I did discover
    How painful love may be;
A maid, mid shades concealing,
Poured forth her voice of feeling,
And love came o'er me stealing,
    She's a dear maid to me!

No. 13.

Several songs both Irish and English are sung to this air, which is well known all over the Munster counties. Nearly all take the name of the air as chorus. Of one, which is full of drollery from beginning to end, I give a single stanza as a specimen. The minstrel, who describes himself as "A young fellow that's airy and bold," philosophises in this fashion about worldly wealth:—

    To quarrel for riches I ne'er was inclined,
    For the greatest of misers must leave them behind;
    I'll buy a milch cow that will never run dry
        And I'll milk her by twisting her horn;
    There was old Paddy Murphy had money galore,
    And Damer of Shronell had twenty times more;
    They are now on their backs under nettles and stones,
        Agus fágamaoid súd mar atá sé!

The last line, which is also the name of the air, is pronounced "*Faugameedh shoodh morra thaushay.*" The "milch cow that will never run dry," means a potteen still; and the twisting of her horn is an allusion to the twisted shape of the *worm*. Damer of Shronell in the county Tipperary, was the Crœsus of the south of Ireland.

14   ANCIENT IRISH MUSIC.

FÁGAMAOID SUD MAR ATÁ SÉ.   LET US LEAVE THAT AS IT IS.   ♩ = pend. 16 inches.

No. 14.

The words "Ace and deuce" (or one and two) mean here the highest pitch of excellence; and as the name indicates, the tune was considered the perfection of music when well played on the bag-pipes, and its correct performance was believed to be a sufficient test of the instrumental skill of a piper. It belongs to the class of "set dances," a term which is explained in the Preface. I noted it down in 1853 from the whistling of John Dolan, of Glenosheen in the county Limerick.

AON IS DÓ NA PIOBAIREACHTA. THE ACE AND DEUCE OF PIPERING. Set Dance.

Horn-pipe time.

No. 15.

Taken down in 1854 from the singing of Peggy Cudmore, of Glenosheen, in the county Limerick, a little girl of about thirteen years of age. A few of our airs, though in the minor scale, end in the tonic of the relative major. The air of Moore's song, "Silent, O Moyle," is an example; and the present air is another. One stanza of the song will be sufficient:—

> 'Tis not your gold would me entice
> To marry you against my friends' advice;
> And I never do intend at all
> To be away from my mother's call;
> And I never do intend at all
> To be away from my mother's call!

ANCIENT IRISH MUSIC. 17

No. 16.

From the flute-playing of David Grady, of Ardpatrick, county Limerick.

REEL. 　　　　　　　　　　　　　　　　　𝅗𝅥 = pend. 12 inches.

Lively.

No. 17.

I cannot tell when I learned the air and words of this song, for I have known them as long as my memory can reach back. Some portions of the old song are spirited and well adapted to the air; others are very rude and worthless; and for several reasons it could not be presented to the reader. I give instead, what may be called a new song, in which I have incorporated the best lines of the original, including two verses almost unchanged.

I'M GOING TO BE MARRIED ON SUNDAY.

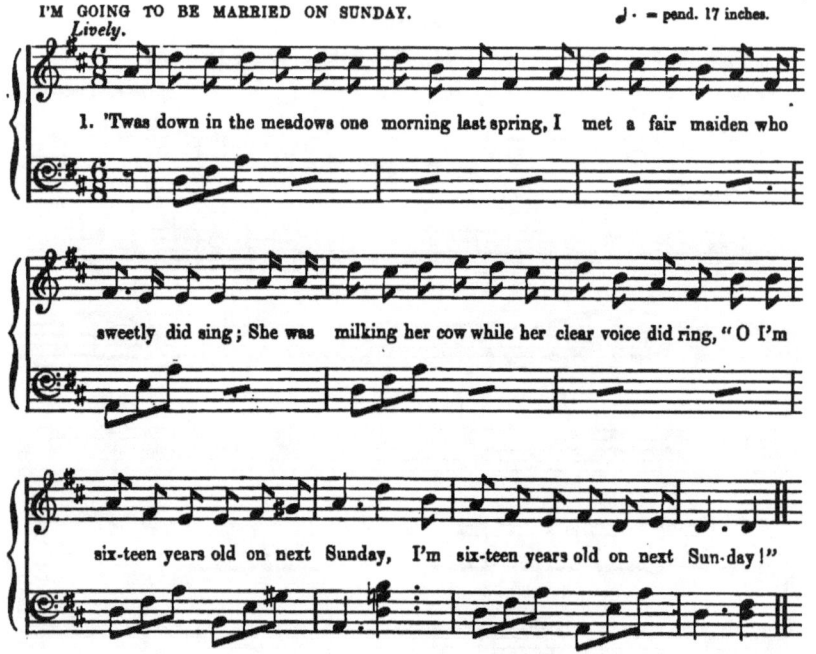

1. 'Twas down in the meadows one morning last spring, I met a fair maiden who sweetly did sing; She was milking her cow while her clear voice did ring, "O I'm sixteen years old on next Sunday, I'm sixteen years old on next Sunday!"

2. 'Tis quite time to marry when a girl is sixteen;
'Twas Willy that told me, so it's plain to be seen;
For he's handsome and manly and fit for a queen,
    And just twenty years old on next Sunday,
    Just twenty years old on next Sunday!

3. On next Sunday morning our wedding shall be,
All the lasses and lads will be present to see;
And oh, how they'll wish to be Willy and me,
    And be married like us on next Sunday,
    Be married like us on next Sunday!

4. My friends say sixteen is too youthful to marry,
And for two or three more they would have me to tarry,
They say it is better my milk-pail to carry,
    And put off my wedding on Sunday,
    And put off my wedding on Sunday.

ANCIENT IRISH MUSIC.

5. But I think my friends have a small share of skill,
   And for two or three more it's against my will;
   It's a promise I made and I must it fulfil,
       And I wish that to-morrow was Sunday,
       I wish that to-morrow was Sunday!

6. On Saturday night when I'm free from all care,
   I'll finish my dress and I'll paper my hair;
   There are three pretty maidens to wait on me there,
       And to dance at my wedding on Sunday,
       To dance at my wedding on Sunday!

7. My Willy is loving and faithful to me,
   And this very next Sunday our wedding shall be;
   Oh, my heart's full of joy, and I'm frantic with glee,
       When I think of my wedding on Sunday,
       When I think of my wedding on Sunday!

No. 18.

This air belongs to the same class as No. 8—page 8. I took down both air and words in 1853, from the singing of John Hennesy, of Kilfinane in the county Limerick.

√ THE SUMMER IS COME AND THE GRASS IS GREEN.   ♪ • =pend. 24 inches.

Slow and with expression.

ANCIENT IRISH MUSIC.

The summer is come and the grass is green,
The leaves are budding on ev'ry tree,
The ships are sailing upon the sea,
And I'll soon find tidings of gramachree.

The night was stormy and wet and cold.
When I lost my darling, my true love bold;
I'll range the valleys and mountains high,
And I'll never marry until I die.

O Johnny, Johnny, I love you well,
I love you better than tongue can tell;
I love my friends and relations too,
But I'd leave them all love, and go with you!

No. 19.

Taken down in 1847, from the whistling of William Sheedy, of Fanningstown, in the county Limerick.

ANCIENT IRISH MUSIC. 21

No. 20.

I learned this beautiful air from my father; and I remember a part of the song, of which I give the first verse. As far as I recollect, each stanza except the first ended with the line "All on the mountains high." Pomeroy is in the county Tyrone; but I have heard the song sung by others, whose version was "two miles below Fermoy." (Co. Cork). The word "below" refers, I believe, not to elevation, but to direction (north or south), in accordance with a custom very general in Ireland.

  As I roved out one evening two miles below Pomeroy,
  I met a farmer's daughter all on the mountains high;
  I said, "my pretty fair maid your beauty shines so clear,
  Upon these lonely mountains, I'm glad to meet you here."

THE MOUNTAINS HIGH.

No. 21.

In the same manner as languages are gradually changed by those who use them, so also it is with popular music. Great numbers of our airs have various "settings" as we call them, which differ sometimes only very slightly, and sometimes so considerably, that one is occasionally in doubt whether they come from the same original, or are different airs altogether. We may imagine that such changes were often the result of incorrect transmission from one player or singer to another; while in other cases, they were made deliberately as improvements, by fiddlers, pipers, or singers,—each change slight in itself—but without any intention of altering the whole into what might be called a different melody. And it is easy to understand, what indeed has not unfrequently happened, that in this manner an air might in course of time, be altered gradually and almost insensibly, note by note as it were, so as ultimately to become nearly unrecognisable.

But it will I think appear clear to any one who studies the subject attentively, that sometimes airs were changed in a totally different way; that occasionally some skilful musician deliberately altered an air all at once, with the direct intention of converting it into a different melody altogether. This he accomplished by altering the time, the rate of movement, the relative length of the notes, or the mode (major to minor or *vice versa*), or by differently combining the several phrases; and not unfrequently all these changes were made in one melody. Two airs related to each other in this manner, have usually nearly the same intervals, a more or less similar succession of notes of the scale, and a general resemblance of strain throughout; but they are so unlike in other respects, that they commonly pass off as different melodies, and their common origin can only be detected by close and critical observation. Bunting asserted, in his Preface to "The Ancient Melodies of Ireland," that an air, once impressed on the popular ear, is unchangeable; an assertion utterly groundless, as every one knows who has the least knowledge of popular music. Its fallacy is fully exposed by Mr. George Farquhar Graham, in his "Introduction" to "Wood's Songs of Scotland," and by Dr. Petrie, in his "Ancient Music of Ireland."

I will now give some examples of airs which have obviously a common source, one being derived from the other, or both from the same original melody; but I will observe that in cases of this kind, it is not always possible to pronounce by which of the two influences described above, the change has been effected.

The four airs which follow were procured in the same neighbourhood; and I think no reasonable doubt can be entertained that they are all varieties of the same melody.

The first I noted down from the singing of Michael Dinneen, a farmer living in Coolfree, on the borders of Cork and Limerick. I also took down some stanzas of a sad Irish song which he sang to it, said to have been composed by a young widowed bride, whose husband had been drowned in conveying her relations in a boat across the Shannon, after the wedding.

AN CUMHAIN LEATSA AN ÓIDHCHE ÚD? DO YOU REMEMBER THAT NIGHT?

No. 22.

I took down this with one stanza of the song, from Lewis O'Brien, a farmer, living also in Coolfree; and it will be perceived that it differs from the preceding chiefly in rhythm, and in the position of the accent. Cappadanig is obviously the name of a place.

CEAPACH-DÁINIG. CAPPADANIG.

Mo mhíle slán chúghat a Cheapach-dainig,
Anois go bráth agus go négad;
Mar is minic a d'fhágbhais a d-tigh an tábhairne
Am' amadán gan chéill me.

Lá'r namhárach bhídhin dúbhach, tinn, cásmluir,
  'Gus ná'r bh'feas dam cad do dhéanfainn;
"Na'r neartaigh an tard-Mhac ná Righ na ngrás leat;"
  Ba shé súd rádh mo chéile.

My thousand farewells to you, O Cappadanig
  Now for ever, and until I die;
For twas often you left me in the tavern,
  As a fool without my reason.
On the morrow I would be melancholy, sick, and sorry,
  And would n't know what I should do;
"May neither the high Son nor the King of mercy strengthen you;"
  That is what my wife would say to me.

No. 23.

Taken down in 1853, from the singing of Joseph Martin (see p. 5); it is commonly known both in Munster and in Connaught by the name given here. This air differs considerably from the two preceding; but the general resemblance is too close I think, to admit of the supposition that it had an independent origin.

THE GREEN BUSHES.

No. 24.

I noted this air in 1853, from the singing of Mrs. Cudmore, who then lived at Glenosheen in the connty Limerick. The chief peculiarity that distinguishes it from the others is the minor mode but in other respects it does not differ materially from the first (No. 21).

No. 25.

I cannot believe that the two following airs were composed independently of each other; for their structure is exactly similar, and some of the straius are identical. The difference seems however too great to be accounted for by accident, or by gradual divergence; and it is probable that the first was formed from the second by some one skilful hand. I learned both in early days from my father. To the first there were English words—a song of 1798—every verse of which ended with the chorus:—

"We are the boys of Wexford, our equals can't be found,
"And our fame like a comet goes through the world round."

WE ARE THE BOYS OF WEXFORD.

No. 26.

I remember three stanzas of a song to this air. The conception and plan are good, but two of the verses are too coarse for publication; and even the one I give had to be softened down in one particular word.

"Whistle, whistle, daughter, and you must get a cow,"
"Oh, no, no, no, no, mother, I will not have her now;
"It is well known,
"I am a woman grown;
"More's the pity one so pretty as I should live alone!"

I will give the song in a new dress. The three verses are retained, as little altered as possible; and even the old rhymes are preserved. I have endeavoured also to carry out the original spirit and conception.

2. "Cheer up, cheer up, daughter, and you shall get a lamb!"
"Oh, if that's the news, dear mother, I'll stay just as I am;
"My little sister May,
"Can take the lamb away,
But I'm quite a woman now, dear mother, and with toys I cannot play."

3. "Cheer up, cheer up, daughter, and you shall get a sheep!"
   "Oh, no, no, no, dear mother, it would not let me sleep;
   "With lambs or sheep I ne'er
   "Could rid my head of care;
   "To feed and tend them day by day is more than I could bear."

4. "Cheer up, cheer up, daughter, and you shall get a cow!
   "Oh, no, no, no, dear mother, I cannot cheer up now;
   "To our neighbours 'tis well known
   "I'm quite a woman grown,
   "And they say 'tis pity one so pretty as I should live alone!"

5. "Cheer up, cheer up, daughter, and married you shall be!"
   "Oh, I'll cheer up now, dear mother, for that's the news for me!"
   "You're a silly maid I vow,
   "And why do you cheer up now?"
   "Because I love a young man, dear mother, more than lamb, or sheep, or cow!"

No. 27.

Of the airs that follow, it appears to me that the second is merely an instrumental setting of the first, which as being the simpler, is probably the older form. The first I have known from childhood; the second I took down in 1853, from the whistling of Joseph Martin, already spoken of (p. 5).

In Ireland whenever any very tragic occurrence takes place, such as a wreck, an execution, an accidental drowning, &c. some local poet generally composes a "Lamentation" on the event, which is printed on sheets, and sung by professional ballad singers through towns, and at fairs and markets. I have a great many of these sheets, and there is usually a rude engraving at top suitable to the subject—the figure of a man hanging, a coffin, a skull and cross bones, &c. The lamentation for a criminal is commonly written in the first person, and is supposed to be the utterance of the culprit himself immediately before execution; it is in fact an imaginary "last dying speech." I cannot find one of them worthy of preservation; but the two following stanzas, selected from different lamentations, will serve as characteristic specimens*

"Come all you tender Christians, I hope you will draw near,
"A doleful lamentation, I mean to let you hear;
"How a child of only ten years old did swear our lives away,
"May the Lord have mercy on our souls against the Judgment Day!"

---

* A good specimen, printed in full, will be found in Charles Gavan Duffy's "Ballad Poetry of Ireland."

"It was a cruel murder, the truth I now must own;
"Twas Satan strongly tempted me, as we were both alone;
"Then with a heavy hatchet I gave Connolly a fall,
"And I cut him up in pieces, which appeared the worst of all."

They are nearly all sung to the following air—at least in the south of Ireland; and of course they are composed in the same measure. I have repeatedly heard Lamentations sung to this air through the streets of Dublin.

LAMENTATION AIR.

No. 28.
(See Notice to No. 27.)

NA MNÁ DEASA AN BHAILE-LOCHA-RIABHACH. THE PRETTY LASSES OF LOUGHREA.

No. 29.

The two fine melodies that follow will be at once perceived to bear a strong resemblance to each other; but whether they are derived from a common source, or are wholly different, I leave an open question. In expression they are very unlike; the first being slow and full of tenderness; the second bold and animated.

I noted down No. 29. "*Spéir-bhean*" in the year 1852, from the whistling of Davy Condon, a *thatcher* by trade, of Ballyorgan in the county Limerick. The name, which I have translated, "Bright Lady," is compounded of *spéir*, the sky, and *bean*, a woman, and signifies literally "Celestial-woman."

32 ANCIENT IRISH MUSIC.

No. 30.

I took down this tune in 1854, from the singing of my grandmother, who was then upwards of ninety years of age; and she informed me that she learned it in her childhood. There was an Irish song to it which she once knew, but had then quite forgotten. From the character and structure and bold expression of the air, I think it likely that it was used as a march tune. The name also, which commemorates an unhappy phase in the history of our country, would seem to afford some confirmation of this opinion. "*Shanavest*" signifies an old vest, and "*Caravat*," a cravat; and they are well known in the south and south-east of Ireland, as the names of two hostile factions, who fought against each other at fairs, markets, and meetings of all kinds, in the last century. We have had also such faction designations as "Black-feet" and "White-feet," "Three years old" and "Four years old," &c. When I was a boy I often witnessed a furious fight with sticks and stones, between "Three years" and "Four years," at the fairs of Ardpatrick and Kildorrery; and I regret to add that these factions and their quarrels are not yet quite extinct in my native county. But if we owe the beautiful melody that follows to faction fighting, it is a consolation to reflect that the practice has not passed away without leaving behind it some compensation for the injury it inflicted on the country.

THE SHANAVEST AND CARAVAT.   A Faction Tune

No. 31.

The term "Single Jig" will be found explained in the Preface. This spirited tune has remained in my memory since I was a child; and I could hardly help learning it, for it was a general favourite with fiddlers, pipers, and dancers.

ANCIENT IRISH MUSIC.

No. 32.

Learned from my father. I heard it also in 1858 among the miners at the head of Glenmalure in the county Wicklow, where I found it was well known, and a favourite dancing tune.

BEALLTAINE. (pron. Beltina.) MAY DAY. HORNPIPE.

ANCIENT IRISH MUSIC.

No. 33.

Taken down in 1853 from the whistling of Joseph Martin a native of the county Limerick.

SLÁN AGUS BEANNACHT LE BUAIRIDHIBH A' TSAOGHAIL
FAREWELL TO THE TROUBLES OF THE WORLD.

36   ANCIENT IRISH MUSIC.

No. 34.

I noted down this fine air in the year 1852 from the whistling of a native of Crossmolina in the county Mayo; and its origin may with great probability be assigned to that very musical county. It will be observed that it has the peculiarity noticed in connexion with No. 15, namely, that it is in the minor mode, but terminates on the relative major.

No. 35.

To this air, which I learned long ago from my father, there was a song beginning with the words "How do you like her for your wife?" but it is not worth printing. I give instead, a song of my brother's, composed expressly to suit the air.*

---

* From "Ballads of Irish Chivalry," by Robert Dwyer Joyce, M.D., M.R.I.A. Dublin, James Duffy; Boston, Patrick Donahoe.

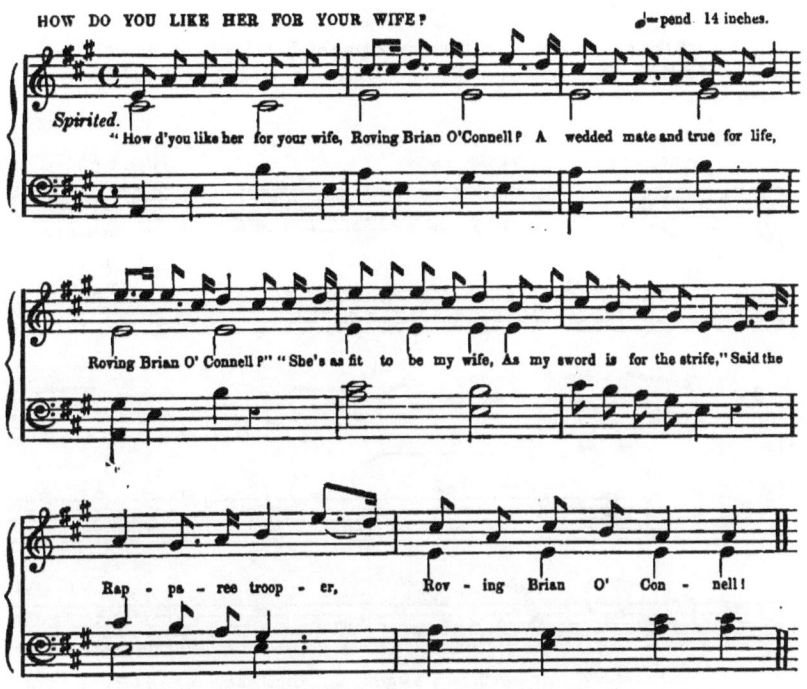

"Ne'er to Mabel prove untrue, Roving Brian O'Connell,
"For O, she'd die for love of you, Roving Brian O'Connell."
    "O, my wild heart never knew
    "A love so warm and constant too,"
Said the Rapparee trooper, Roving Brian O'Connell!

* * * * * * *

"How will you your young bride keep, Roving Brian O'Connell?
"The foeman's bands are ne'er asleep, Roving Brian O'Connell."
    "In our hold by Counal's steep,
    "Who dare make my Mabel weep?"
Said the Rapparee trooper, Roving Brian O'Connell.

"This day in ruined church you stand, Roving Brian O'Connell,
"To take your young bride's priceless hand, Roving Brian O'Connell."
    "O, my heart, my arm, and brand,
    "Are for her and our dear land,"
Said the Rapparee trooper, Roving Brian O'Connell.

No. 36.

I noted this fine tune in 1851, from the singing of John Dinan, of Glenanair, in the county Limerick. I also took down the Irish song, every verse of which ended with the name of the air as chorus.

FAGHAIM ARÍS A' CRUISCÍN AS BIODH SÉ LÁN. WE'LL TAKE AGAIN A CRUISKÉEN, A CRUISKEEN LAUN.

No. 37.

This Tune belongs to the class of "Set dances," (*see Preface*). It was a great favourite twenty or thirty years ago in some of the Munster counties; and I learned it from hearing it constantly played by pipers and fiddlers.

THE JOB OF JOURNEYWORK. A Set dance.

No. 38.

This plaintive air is well known all over the south of Ireland; and the song, "*Drahareen-O-Machree*," which has given it a name, is heard everywhere among the people. I have known both air and words since my childhood; and the words are still printed on broadsheets. Here is the first stanza:—

"I am a young fellow that always loved rural sport;
"The fairs and the patrons of Erin I used to resort;
"The true sons of Bacchus were always my companie,
"Until I was deprived of my Drahareen-O-Machree!"

ANCIENT IRISH MUSIC.

There was an older song to this air, called "Jemmy, Mo-veela-sthore" (Jemmy, my thousand treasures), of which I give one verse with the music.

DRAHAREEN-O-MACHREE. LITTLE BROTHER OF MY HEART.

No. 39.

The song which has given name to this air—beginning "The very first day I left Carrick," is still printed on sheets, and sung by ballad-singers in the southern counties.

THE LOVELY SWEET BANKS OF THE SUIR.

No. 41.

I noted this fine characteristic old melody, in the summer of 1853, from the singing of Alice Kenny, an old woman living in the parish of Glenroe, in the county Limerick. I also wrote down the words of the Irish song, which is one of those Jacobite allegorical compositions, that were so common in Ireland in the early part of the last century; but I afterwards found several copies of it in the Library of the Royal Irish Academy: and it has been published by Mr. John O'Daly, in his " Poets and Poetry of Munster," (Second Series page 7,) with a metrical translation by " Erionnach." The air however, is now published for the first time.

I cannot forbear recalling the circumstances under which I obtained this air. I had often heard of old Alice Kenny, who was at this time about 70 years of age, as a noted singer in her time; and I set out one day to visit her. When I arrived at her house, her grandchildren told me, she was up somewhere on the neighbouring hill; so I and my companion set out in search of her; and we found her on the very top, pulling heath to cook her supper. We sat down by a turf-rick, and there for two hours, she delighted me and delighted herself, with her inexhaustible store of Irish airs and songs of all kinds,—love songs, *keens*, lullabies, execution songs, &c. I took down several, and left her, determined to renew my visit at the first opportunity. But no opportunity came; and I have never seen poor old Alice from that day to this.

AN CEÓ DRAOIGHEACHTA. THE MAGIC MIST.

No. 41.

Learned from my father.

THE BAG OF MEAL. Jig.   ♩. = pend. 10 inches.

No. 42.

I noted this tune from the singing of Joseph Martin (see page 5); but it is well known in Munster; and the song, of which I give the second verse with the music, still continues to be printed on broadsides.

THE SHAMROCK SHORE.

No. 43.

I learned this air in my childhood; I remember also a few lines of the song, but they are quite unworthy of preservation.

THE WEE WEE BAG OF *PRATIES*. ♩ = pend. 10 inches.

No. 44.

I cannot tell when I learned this air; I have known both tune and words longer than my memory can reach back.

THERE WAS A BOLD BEGGARMAN. ♩ = pend. 10 inches.

No. 45.

The Irish song to this air is a kind of mock lament uttered by the person from whom the little bag was stolen. He begins with the words "Ullulu mo mháilín, mo mháilín, do goideadh uaim," "Alas, my little bag, my little bag that was stolen from me!" A second person asks, "What was in your little bag, your little bag that was stolen from you?" and this gives the victim an opportunity of detailing all the precious contents of the little bag—a most whimsical enumeration:—a lot of fine clothes—meal and flour—two or three potatoes—honey, wax, and cheese—butter and apples—a flitch of bacon—Paddy's stockings, Shaneen's brogues, &c. &c.

In the whole range of Irish airs, there is scarcely one more universally known in Munster than this. It bears a resemblance to "Fag-a-ballagh," the air of Moore's song "To ladies' eyes a round, boys;" but it is undoubtedly a distinct melody.

ANCIENT IRISH MUSIC. 47

No. 46.

I noted down this fine air in 1853, from the singing of Michael Dinneen, of Coolfree, county Limerick. The burden "Ben-erinn í," is common to several love songs. The best I have seen is one written by a poet of the last century, William Heffernan, or Blind William, as he is more usually called, a native of Shronell in Tipperary. It was published by Edward Walsh, with a metrical translation, in his "Irish Popular Songs." I give the last stanza of his translation with the air.

BÉ N-EIRINN Í. (pron. Bain-airing-ee), WHOE'ER SHE BE.

No. 47.

I took down this fine tune in 1852, from Lewis O'Brien of Coolfree in the county Limerick; who stated that More was the guardian fairy of Cloyne in Cork. We read in Irish History of several remarkable women named Mór (pron. More). The most celebrated of all was Mor Mumhan, the daughter of Aedh Bennain (Hugh Bannan, king of west

Munster — died A.D. 614), about whom there is a curious story in the book of Leinster; in which it is related that she was carried off by the fairies in her youth; and that ultimately she became the wife of Cathal Mac Finguine, king of Cashel. Afterwards her sister was similarly abducted; and was discovered by Mór—who knew her by her singing,—somewhere in the district where Cloyne is situated.

Mór Mumhan (or Mór of Munster) is celebrated in legend among the peasantry to this day, for her beauty and her adventures; and perhaps it may not be rash to conjecture that she was the same as Mór of Cloyne, who gave name to this air.

MÓR CHLUANA. MORE OF CLOYNE.

No. 48.

THE TOP OF CORK ROAD. JIG.

No. 49.

Learned from my father. The song which begins. "Of all the men that's breathing a rover is my delight," describes the rambles of a man who travelled through all the principal towns of Ireland, and worked at a different trade in every town—"Changing his occupation in ev'ry place that's new." It does not possess sufficient merit to warrant me in printing it; but I give one verse with the music.

ROVING JACK OF ALL TRADES.

No. 50.

We have in Ireland several hunting songs, each describing the events of some particular chase; such as "The Kilruddery hunt," and the "County Limerick Buck-Hunt," both published by Crofton Croker, in his Popular Songs of Ireland; and I have copies of others. The song of "Reynard the Fox" has long been a favourite; and to the present day continues to be printed as a street ballad. The old people of the Midland counties still retain some traditions of this great hunt, which, according to my version of the song, took place in 1793. I learned the air and words from my father; but the version now commonly printed on sheets is a little different, for both date and names are altered to suit a later time. All the versions that I have seen or heard agree in the line "Arklow and Wicklow along the sea shore," which appears absurd, as these two places lie far out of the line of the chase. It is probably a corruption. The fox making his will is a piece of drollery which has its parallel elsewhere; for they have in England "The hunting of the hare, with her last will and testament." (Chappell, Popular Music of the Olden Time; p. 321).

REYNARD THE FOX. A Hunting Song. ♩ = pend. 13 inches.
With spirit.

The first day of spring in the year ninetythree, The first recreation was in this counterie; The King's county gentlemen o'er hills, dales & rocks, They rode out so jovially in search of a fox. Tally-ho hark-away, Tally-ho hark-away, Tally-ho hark-away, My boys, away, hark-away!

When Reynard was started he faced Tullamore,
Arklow and Wicklow along the sea-shore;
We kept his brush in view ev'ry yard of the way,
And he straight took his course through the street of Roscrea! Tally-ho, &c.

But Reynard, sly Reynard, lay hid there that night,
And they swore they would watch him until the day-light;
Early next morning the woods they did resound
With the echo of horns and the sweet cry of hounds. Tally-ho, &c.

When Reynard was started he faced to the hollow,
Where none but the hounds and footmen could follow;
The gentlemen cried "Watch him, watch him, what shall we do?
"If the rocks do not stop him he will cross Killaloe!" Tally-ho, &c.

When Reynard was taken, his wishes to fulfil,
He called for ink and paper, and pen to write his will;
And what he made mention of, they found it no blank,
For he gave them a cheque on the national bank. Tally-ho, &c.

"To you, Mr. Casey, I give my whole estate;
"And to you, young O'Brien, my money and my plate;
"And I give to you, Sir Francis, my whip, spurs and cap,
"For you crossed walls and ditches and ne'er looked for a gap!" Tally-ho, &c.

No. 51.

I noted down this reel from Ned Goggin, who has been the professional fiddle-player of Glenosheen in the county Limerick, from the time of my childhood to the present day.

No. 52.

Dr. Petrie has given, in his "Ancient Music of Ireland," a setting of this tune, obtained from the county Kilkenny, with the name of "Ree Raw." The tune is well known in Cork and Limerick, and I learned it when a boy from fiddlers and pipers, who used to play it as a "set dance." I remember seeing a man dance it one time on a table. As the Munster version differs very considerably from that published by Dr. Petrie, I have thought it better to give it. It is worthy of remark, that the Munster name of this tune (Kimel-a-vauleen, as it is pronounced) is used, like "Ree Raw," to signify confusion or uproarious merriment.

CUMAIL A' MHAILIN. RUB THE BAG. A Set dance.

ANCIENT IRISH MUSIC.   53

No. 53.

Taken down from the whistling of James Quain and of Michael Dinneen, both of Coolfree, (see pp. 3 and 23). This was the marching tune of the family of the O'Donovans, who were anciently the chiefs of the territory of Hy Fidhgheinte, a district lying west of the river Maigue in the county Limerick.

FEAD AN IOLAIR. THE EAGLE'S WHISTLE.

No. 54.

I learned this beautiful and characteristic melody from my father. Of the Irish song I retain only a few fragments, which are not worth preserving. Perhaps the reader will be better pleased if I give instead a song of my brother's, composed to suit the air.*

AN CIARRAIGHEACHT MALLUIGHTHE. THE WICKED KERRYMAN.

* From "Ballads of Irish Chivalry," by Robert D. Joyce, M.D., M.R I.A.
Dublin, James Duffy; Boston, Patrick Donahoe.

There on my rocky throne, my Eveleen,
Ever, ever alone, my Eveleen,
    I sit dreaming of thee;
High on the fern-clad rocks reclining there,
Though the wild birds their songs are twining fair,
Thee I hear, and I see thy shining hair,
    Still, still, sweet Gragal Machree!

*   *   *   *   *   *

Deeply in broad Kilmore, my Eveleen,
Down by the wild stream's shore, my Eveleen,
    I've made a sweet home for thee;
Yellow and bright, like thy long, long flowing hair,
Flowers the fairest, are ever blowing there,
Fairer still, with thy clear eyes glowing there,
    Fondly, sweet Gragal Machree!

Then come away, away, my Eveleen;
We will spend each day, my Eveleen,
    Blissful and loving and free:
Come to the woods where the streams are pouring blue,
Which the eagle is ever soaring through;
I'll grow fonder each day adoring you,
    There, there, sweet Gragal Machree!

No. 55.

The song to this air is common I believe to England, Ireland and Scotland. It has been long known in the south of Ireland, and is still printed as a street ballad. The English version originated with Tom D'Urfey, a well-known song writer, who died in the beginning of the last century. The old version of the Irish song differs a good deal from it; and it may be questioned which is the original. Both are however low in point of literary merit as well as of morality; and they are not worth disputing about. The air to which the song is sung in England is also claimed by Scotland; and it is published both in Chappell's "Popular Music of the Olden Time," and in Wood's "Songs of Scotland." But the Irish air, which I think very graceful and beautiful, is entirely different; so that we may claim undisputed possession of it. I give it here as I learned it long ago, with one verse of the song. In the last line I have thought it better to substitute the words in italics for those in the original.

COLD AND ROUGH THE NORTH WIND BLOWS.

No. 56.

This jig is universally known in Munster. In some places it is called "O, chailleach, do mharbhais me!"—"O, bag, you have killed me!"

AN TIOCFADH TU A BHAILE LIOM? WILL YOU COME HOME WITH ME?

No. 57.

This spirited air takes its name from the chorus of an Irish drinking song, which I have written phonetically with the music. It may be translated, (First toper)" It is day, it is day, it is day—in the early morning!" (Second toper,)" Arrah, not at all, my dear friend, it is only the light of the moon, shining on high!" There is an English song to the same air (of which I have a full copy on a broad sheet), called "The lamentation of Patrick Keane the tailor," which is full of coarse, broad humour. Here is one half stanza:—

I am a tailor by my trade, in cutting out I am quite handy,
And all I earn ev'ry day, my wife lays out in tea and brandy.

ANCIENT IRISH MUSIC. 59

No. 58.

Noted down in 1852, from James Buckley, a Limerick piper.

KING CHARLES'S JIG. A Set dance.

♩ · ― pend. 10 inches.

Jig time.

No. 59.

Though the custom of employing professional mourners to lament the dead has disappeared from the country; yet in many parts of Ireland the people still join in the cry of sorrow over departed friends; and those among them who possess natural musical abilities, usually modulate their voices to a kind of startlingly wild and pathetic melody.

There are usually in a neighbourhood, two or three women, who are skilled beyond others in *keening*, and who make a practice of attending at wakes and funerals. These often pour forth over the dead person, a lament in Irish—partly extempore, partly prepared—delivered in a kind of plaintive recitative; and at the conclusion of each verse, they lead a choral cry, in which the others who are present join, repeating throughout, "Och-ochone!" or some such words.

The following melody, which I learned long long ago, by repeatedly hearing it, may be considered a very characteristic specimen of these musical burdens. The notes marked with pauses, may be sustained to any length according to the power of voice, or inclination of the singer: I have placed numbers over the pauses, to denote the usual length, in *quavers*, of the prolonged sound. With respect to the concluding note, it is to be observed, that the peasantry, when singing or whistling *keens*, lullabies, or plough tunes, often terminate with a quick and sudden turn upwards from the tonic to the second, fifth or octave.

CAOINE. A KEEN OR LAMENT.

No. 60.

For this air I am indebted to Mr. Charles Morris, of Enniskillen Model School, who heard it sung, and noted it down, in the neighbourhood of that town. I was so impressed with its graceful and playful beauty, that I could not resist the temptation of writing a song to it; and I have tried to make the sentiment of the song correspond with that of the air.

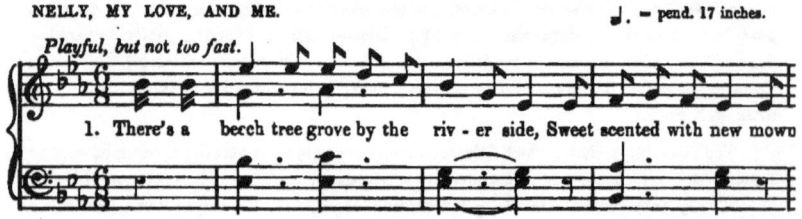

NELLY, MY LOVE, AND ME.

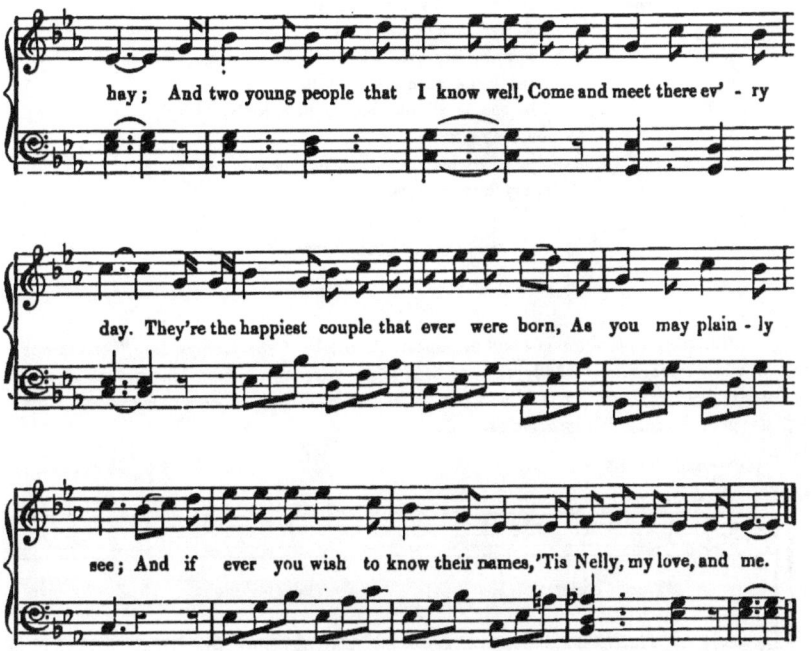

2. There's a sweet little cottage hard by the grove,
    As white as the driven snow;
  And round the windows and up the wall,
    Sweet pea and roses grow;
  'Tis neat and cozy within and without,
    As you may plainly see;
  And that pretty cottage my father built
    For Nelly, my love, and me.

3. Beside the cottage my garden blooms,
    With a hedge of sweet briar all round;
  You never could think of a single flower
    That in it cannot be found.
  And the flowers are laughing like me for joy,
    As you may plainly see;
  For I planted them all with my own two hands,
    For Nelly, my love, and me.

ANCIENT IRISH MUSIC.

4. And I love my Nelly with all my heart,
    Much better than I can tell;
And I know by her eyes when she looks at me,
    That she loves me quite as well.
There's no one at all like my darling Nelly,
    As you may plainly see;
And we're to be married to-morrow morning—
    Nelly, my love, and me.

No. 61.

The song to this air is a sort of lament uttered by "The Croppy Boy," one of the Wexford insurgents of 1798, who had been taken prisoner. I have known both air and words from childhood, and I have a copy of the latter printed on a broad sheet. One stanza of the song will be sufficient.

THE CROPPY BOY.

'Twas early, ear-ly last Thursday night, The Yeoman caval-ry gave me a fright; The fright they gave me was to my down-fall, For I was prisoner ta-ken by Lord Corn-wall.

ANCIENT IRISH MUSIC. 63

No. 62.

No. 63.

I had learned this fine air in my childhood, with a few verses of an English song, the burden of which I have retained as the name of the air. When, about 1852, I began to write down from memory all the airs I had learned in early days, I recollected the first part of this melody, but was unable to recall the second part; for I had neither heard nor sung the tune for very many years. One cold dark evening in November 1852, I was walking through Clanbrassil-street in Dublin; when I heard the air sung sweetly and correctly by a poor woman with a child in her arms; and the first note or two of the second part immediately flashed the whole thing on my memory. I give a song of my brother's composed for the air (See page 54).

ALONG WITH MY LOVE I'LL GO.

My love has an eye of brightness, An arm of valour free; My love has a heart of lightness, But ever true to me The pride of my heart unchanging, His black locks' martial flow, And away to the wild wars ranging, Along with my love I'll go.

> The woods wear winter's sadness,
> And white falls the icy shower.
> There's shelter, peace, and gladness
> Within my father's tower;
> I bore the summer's burning,
> I heed not winter's snow;
> And thus through joy and mourning,
> Along with my love I'll go.

ANCIENT IRISH MUSIC.　　　　　　65

O! ne'er for once to leave him
　In tented field or hall,
To smile if joy receive him,
　Or die if he should fall!
And ever thus unchanging,
　Through want and toil and woe,
Away to the wild wars ranging,
　Along with my love I'll go.

No. 64.

Learned from my father when I was very young. There was a violent political English song to it, the first line of which was, "In comes great Bonaparte with forty-thousand men."

IN COMES GREAT BONAPARTE.

No. 65.

"Bata na bplandaighe" (pron. Bottha na blandy), is understood in Munster to mean a stick for planting cabbages. But Sir William Wilde informs me, that in Connaught the term is applied to a long pointed stick used in setting potatoes; and further that there is a tune of this name known in parts of the west, which was accompanied by an odd sort of dance, a kind of pantomimic representation of the whole process of potato planting. I have not heard this air, and whether it is the same as the one I give here, which I learned from my father, I do not know.

BATA NA BPLANDAIGHE.   THE PLANTING STICK.

No. 66.

The lullaby airs, though sufficiently varied in structure, are all plaintive, and somewhat sad in character; and it will be observed that they resemble in expression the *keens* or laments, and the plough whistles. To many of them there are songs in the Irish language; which have often the same class of ideas running through them:— the baby is soothed to sleep with the promise of a golden cradle (*cliabhán óir*), which is to be hung from the bough of a tree, and rocked by the wind on a fine sunny day, under the shade of the foliage. Dr. Petrie has published one of these in his "Ancient Music of Ireland," (p. 144) to a lullaby air contributed by me. The prevailing idea is perpetuated in the well known nursery rhyme, which has been evidently derived from the Irish words:—

> Huzho-bye, baby, on the tree top;
> When the wind blows the cradle will rock;
> When the bough breaks the cradle will fall—
> Here come down baby, cradle, and all!

When there was no regular song, the air was sung with such words as "Huzho-baby,"—"Sho-heen-sho," &c. continually repeated. I have seen children lulled to sleep hundreds of times with such lullabies; and the following is one of those with which I have been familiar from my childhood.

SUANTRAIDHE (Soontree). LULLABY.

Gently.
Sho-ho, ba - by, Sho-ho, ba-by, Sho-ho ba - by bye;
Sho-ho, ba - by, Sho - ho, ba - by; Sho - ho, ba - by bye.
Sho - ho ba - by bye, Sho - ho ba - by bye.

No. 67.

I learned both the air and the words of this song from my father. It was very well known in my early days among the people of the south; and there are more verses in the song; but those I give are all that I can remember.

FAIR MAIDEN'S BEAUTY WILL SOON FADE AWAY. ♩ = pend. 22 inches.

Andante.

My love she was born in the north coun-te-rie, Where hills and lof-ty mountains rise up from the sea; She's the fair-est young maid-en that e'er I did see, She ex-ceeds all the maids in the north counterie.

My love is as sweet as the cinnamon tree;
She clings to me as close as the bark to the tree:
But the leaves they will wither and the roots will decay,
And fair maiden's beauty will soon fade away!

No. 68.

The song to this air is known also in Scotland; but the Irish and the Scotch versions differ very much in detail. The Scotch song is given in "Wood's Songs of Scotland" (I. 85); and I give here the Irish words (except the few in italics) as I have always heard them sung by the people of Limerick: they have been worked up into a song by my brother—see "Ballads of Irish Chivalry," By R. D. Joyce.—p. 393.

The fifth verse appears to belong to a different song; but it is curious that in the Scotch version there is a corresponding stanza, apparently inconsistent with the rest of the song. So far regarding the words. The Irish air is however quite different from the Scotch; it is well known in Munster; and I have been quite familiar with it all my life.

THE LOWLANDS OF HOLLAND.

With Expression.

The first night I was mar-ried, a hap-py hap-py bride, The captain of the Highlandmen he came to my *lover's* side: "A-rise, a-rise, new married man, a-rise, and come with me, To the Low-lands of Hol-land to face your en-e-my!"

"Holland is a pretty place, most pleasing to be seen,
"The *wild fl·w'rs* grow very plenty there, and vines hang from the trees;
"The *wild flow'rs* grow very plenty there, and vines hang from the trees,"
I scarce had time to look about when my true-love was gone from me.

Says the mother to the daughter, "what makes you so lament?
"Is there no man in Ireland's ground to please your discontent?"
"There are men enough in Ireland, but none at all for me,
"I never loved but one young man, and he is gone from me!"

I ne'er will wear a collar around my neck and hair,
Nor fire bright, nor candle-light shall show my beauty rare;
And I will ne'er get married until the day I die,
Since the raging seas and stormy winds have parted my love and I.

I built my love a gallant ship, a ship of noble fame,
With four-and-twenty seamen bold to steer her across the main:
The storm then began to rise, and the seas began to spout;
'Twas then my love and his gallant ship were sorely tossed about.

No. 69.

We have a class of Irish airs, each phrase of which consists of the unusual number of five bars To this class belong Bunting's air "The Pretty Red Girl," (known in Munster as "Banathee haive"); "The red haired man's wife;" "Drahareen-o-machree," (p. 39 of this book); and many others. Most of them are slow tunes; but a few like the present are quick. Some would perhaps reduce tunes like this to six-eight time, by doubling the length of every fifth bar (which could be done by prolonging the crotchet to the length of five quavers, *i.e.* dotted crotchet and crotchet); but to do so in the present case, would be simply to falsify the tune. The set dance was adapted to it in the way in which I give it here.

No. 70.

Taken down in 1850 from Ned Goggin of Glenosheen, in the county Limerick.

ROUND THE WORLD FOR SPORT. Jig.

No. 71.

A setting of this air has been given in Mr. John O'Daly's "Poets and Poetry of Munster," (2nd ed. p. 70,) with one stanza of an Irish song. My setting, which I noted from James Buckley, a Limerick piper, differs however, so considerably from Mr. O'Daly's, that I think it right to print it.

AN CNUICÍN FRAOIGH.   THE KNOCKEEN-FREE (The Heathy little Hill).   ♩ = pend. 25 inches.

No. 72.

An English friend assures me that he heard the words of the following song many years ago, among the peasantry of the south of England; and he believes the air also to be the one I give here. The mention of nightingales in the first verse points to an English origin, the third verse looks very like Irish manufacture. I sent the air to Mr. Chappell, the great master of English popular music, and he has written to me, saying that he has some faint recollection of having heard it before; and expressing an opinion that it ought to be published. Both the air and the words are well known in the south of Ireland, and I have been acquainted with them as long as I can remember. I think the air is Irish; but I give it here subject to any future claims from other quarters.

I'M A POOR STRANGER AND FAR FROM MY OWN.

As I went a walking one morning in spring, To hear the birds whis-tle and night-in-gales sing; I heard a fair la-dy a-mak-ing great moan, Saying "I'm a poor stranger and far from my own."

And as I drew nigh her I made a low *jee* (bow ?);
I asked her for pardon for making so free;
My heart it relented to hear to her moan,
Saying, "I'm a poor stranger, and far from my own."

* * * * * *

I'll build my love a cottage at the end of this town,
Where lords, dukes and earls shall not pull it down;
If the boys they should ask you what makes you live alone,
You can tell them you're a stranger and far from your own.

No. 73.

I have been all my life familiar with this lullaby; but I have never heard it sung with any words except "Shoheen-sho u-lo-lo shoheen-sho as thu mo-lannav." (Shoheen-sho and you are my child).

SUANTRAIDHE. (Soontree). LULLABY.

No. 74.

This is an air whose nationality it is difficult to determine. A version of it has been printed in Chappell's "Popular Music of the olden time," (p. 522,) under the name of "The Willow tree," which has been long known in England; and the Scotch setting is given in "Wood's Songs of Scotland," (p. 84.) The air is universally known in the south of Ireland, and I give it here as the people sing it. The Irish setting is very like the Scotch, but differs in a few characteristic notes; the English varies considerably from both. As it is with the air, so with the words; the English, Scotch and Irish versions all differ from each other in detail, but have a general resemblance sufficient to prove that they have had a common origin. I give two verses as the people of the south of Ireland sing them; and I know two others, which would scarcely bear publication; but they have the play on the words "thyme" and "rue" the same as the English and Scotch versions.

COME ALL YOU MAIDS WHERE'ER YOU BE.

When I was a maid both fair and young, I flourished in my prime, prime, 'Till a pro-per tall young man came in, And stole this heart of mine, mine, And stole this heart of mine.

The gardener's son being standing by,
Three gifts he gave to me, me,
The pink, the rue, the violet blue,
And the red, red rosy tree, tree,
The red, red rosy tree.

No. 75.

An indifferent setting of this fine melody, under the name of "The Maid of Castle-craigh," was published in 1842, in "The Native Music of Ireland." I give here what I believe to be a much superior setting, as I have heard it sung from my earliest days among the people of Limerick.

I have a full copy of the song—subject, a voyage to America and a narrow escape from shipwreck, with "Captain Thompson;" and I give the last stanza with the music.

CAPTAIN THOMPSON.

ANCIENT IRISH MUSIC. 77

No. 76.

The words of the following Lullaby were composed by Owen Roe O'Sullivan, a Munster poet of the last century; and they are still well known among the Irish-speaking people of Cork and Limerick. They were published by Edward Walsh, with a metrical translation, in his Irish Popular Songs. My own translation of the first verse is here given with the music. I took down the air in 1853, from Davy Condon, already mentioned at page 31. It has not much of the usual character of Lullaby tunes.

SUANTRAIDHE (Soontree). LULLABY.

Gentle movement.
Sho-ho ba-by, weep no more, Thou'lt get what none e'er got before; Each gem thy roy-al fathers wore, When Conn and Owen the sceptre bore. Sho-ho ba-by, weep no more, Sho-ho *lenniv a-chreese asthore!* In sor-row deep I grieve a-lone, For thine eyes in tears, thy hun-gry moan.

No. 77.

There was a lively song to this air; but the following fragment is all that I am able to recall.

(N.B. The "Gorey Caravan" was one of Bianconi's cars that used to travel to and from the town of Gorey in Wexford).

"I met a pretty girl with a bundle in her hand,
"She was going to the New harbour to the Gorey caravan."

THE GOREY CARAVAN.

No. 78.

The English and Scotch have each a ballad named Barbara Allen; and the words of the two ballads, though differing considerably, are only varieties of the same original. Goldsmith, in his second essay, after speaking of the pleasant retirement of his early life, says:—" The Music of the finest singer is dissonance to what I felt when our old dairy-maid sung me into tears with Johnny Armstrong's last good night, or the cruelty of Barbara Allen." These words would lead to the belief that a version of Barbara Allen was current in the midland counties of Ireland, in the time of Goldsmith's childhood; and this belief receives some confirmation from the fact that I have heard the ballad among the peasantry of Limerick. In the year 1847 a young girl named Ellen Ray, of Glenroe, in the county of Limerick, sang it for me, with such power and feeling, that the air became at once stereotyped on my memory. I did not take a copy of the words, which I now regret very much; but I remember two lines, which vary from the corresponding lines in the English and Scotch versions:—

"And every toll that the death-bell gave
Was "I died for you *Barbary Ellen*."

The air to which the ballad is sung in England is quite different from that which they have in Scotland: the Irish air differs from both, and may I think, compare favourably with either.

No. 79.

I learned this air in my boyhood; and I heard a song to it beginning with the line "Young Roger was a ploughboy both buxom and gay;" but it is not fit for publication. I give a song of my brother's (see page 54), composed for the air. (N.B. I have slightly altered a few of the lines, the better to suit the song to the proper setting of the air. I have done this on my own responsibility, as there was no time to communicate with the author across the Atlantic.)

Air:—YOUNG ROGER WAS A PLOUGHBOY.   ♩ = pend. 16 inches.
With animation.

Young John-ny in the autumn to Lim'rick he came, And none knew what brought him, and none knew his name; But he court-ed Bes-sie Gray On that sun-ny au-tumn day, And he told her sweet ro-man-ces 'mid the new mown hay. Then

Chorus.

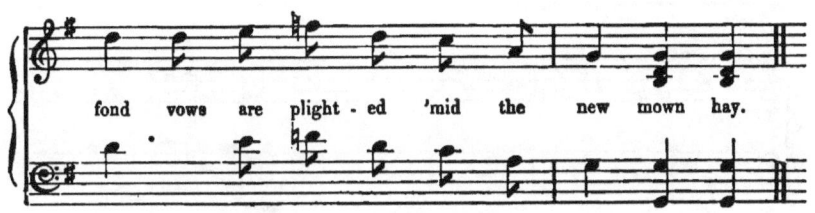

2. When ere the next sweet morning young Johnny had fled,
With envy filled and scorning, the village maidens said,—
Oh, they spoke of Bessie Gray,
And they said she'd rue the day,
When she heard the sweet romances 'mid the new-mown hay.
Chorus—Then Oh! for fields lighted, &c.

3. Young Johnny's happy dwelling lay fast by the Lee;
And in manly parts excelling, but few like him you'd see;
And so thought Bessie Gray,
On that sunny autumn day,
When she heard the sweet romances 'mid the new-mown hay. *Chorus.*

4. Young Johnny could remember his vows and his flame;
He came in December, and all knew his name;
And there was a wedding gay
And the bride was Bessie Gray
And all from these romances 'mid the new-mown hay. *Chorus.*

No. 80.

Noted down from the whistling of Philip Gleeson, of Coolfree, in the county of Limerick.

THE FIELD OF HAY. ne.

♩. = pend. 10 inches.

No. 81.

I am not aware that the following tune has been published in any musical collection; but it is printed in the "Ordnance Memoir of Londonderry," where however, it is practically inaccessible to the general public, as that book is very scarce. It has long been appropriated as the marching tune at the yearly celebration of the shutting and opening of the gates of Derry; and its use has with great probability descended from the period of the siege itself.

It is a very fine old Irish melody, bearing all the marks of an antiquity far beyond that of the siege. It is well known in some parts of Ulster, but scarcely known at all in the other provinces; and this fact, together with its historic interest, will I hope be considered a sufficient justification for publishing, in this one instance, a tune that has been printed already.

NO SURRENDER.

No. 82.

Noted down in 1853, from James Buckley, a Limerick piper already frequently mentioned.

TEA IN THE MORNING. Hop Jig.

No. 83.

Taken down in 1854, from the whistling of Joseph Martin, whom I have already frequently mentioned in connexion with other tunes.

IT IS TO FAIR ENGLAND I'M WILLING TO GO.

No. 84.

I took down this air and the song in connexion with it, from Peggy Cudmore (see page 16), a little girl gifted with extraordinary natural musical talent, from whom I also got several other tunes. The song is still well known in Munster; but in its current form its language is very feeble, as well as defective in rhythmical correctness. It is however so full of genuine fun and good humour, that I thought it a pity not to preserve it. Accordingly

I have clipped, patched, added, and amended—dressed it up in a new suit; so that I fear old acquaintances will hardly recognise it. But the original spirit is faithfully preserved. (N.B. *Sprissaun* means an insignificant fellow, quite beneath notice.)

THE GAME PLAYED IN ERIN-GO-BRAGH.

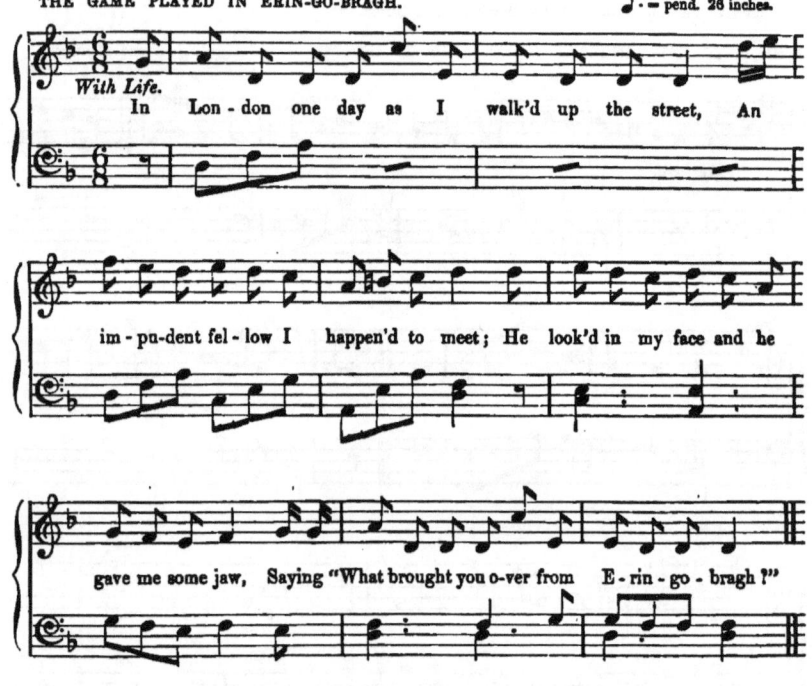

In London one day as I walk'd up the street, An impudent fellow I happen'd to meet; He look'd in my face and he gave me some jaw, Saying "What brought you over from E-rin-go-bragh?"

"I know you're a Paddy by the blink of your eye,
"Your crimes and misconduct have forced you to fly;
"You left your own country for breaking the law,
"And escaped from the gallows in Erin-go-bragh!"

The blackthorn stick that I held in my fist,
Around his big body I gave it a twist;
I silenced his tongue with a whack on the jaw,
And I showed him the game played in Erin-go-bragh.

They all gathered round me like a flock of wild geese—
"Is this Irish Paddy disturbing the peace?
"We'll march him to prison for breaking the law,
"This quarrelsome villain from Erin-go-bragh."

"To the —— I pitch ye, ye set of *Sprissauns*,
"For here comes Jack Murphy from Ballyknockaun,
"With my mother's first cousin, Mick Ryan from Dunlaw,
"And big Paddy Kelly from Erin-go-bragh!"

Oh, the scrimmage we had—'twould delight you to see!
Mavrone, how we shook our shillelahs with glee!
We leathered them well, and we laughed at their law,
And we showed them the game played in Erin-go-bragh!

No. 87.

THE BLOOMING MEADOWS. Jig. ♩ = pend. 10 inches.

No. 86.

This tune is well known, and extremely popular in the counties of Dublin, Wicklow, Wexford, and Carlow; and I think not without good reason, for it appears to me to be a surpassingly beautiful melody, and most characteristically Irish. I have often heard it sung and played by itinerant musicians, in the streets of Dublin. Ballymanus is in the county Wicklow. I have a different setting of the air, which I took down many years ago from Joseph Martin (see page 5), and which he knew by the name of "The Banks of sweet Loughrea;" but it is in every respect inferior to the Leinster setting given here.

BILLY BYRNE OF BALLYMANUS.   ℭ = pend. 20 inches.

No. 87.

Taken down in 1853, from James Buckley (see p. 11).

THE LITTLE HORSE TIED AT A PUBLIC HOUSE.

Moderate time.

No. 88.

The following fine melody is a good illustration of the remark already made regarding the resemblance that often exists between lullubies and *keens* or laments; for if the reader had not been told beforehand that this is a lullaby, he would perhaps find it difficult to determine to which of the two classes it belongs. I noted it down from the singing of Davy Condon, already mentioned in connexion with No. 29. The last or tonic note was prolonged *ad libitum* with the words " Huzh-o, huzh-o," continually repeated.

SUARTRAIDHE. (Soontree). LULLABY.

Slowly and Gently.

Huzh - o.

No. 89.

I learned this spirited air in early days from my father; and I know the greater part of an English song to it; but it is not fit for publication. The song I give is one of my brother's (see p. 54).

Air:—THERE WAS AN OLD ASTROLOGER.   ♩ = pend. 22 inches.

With animation.

My wild heart's love, my woodland dove, The ten-der and the true, She dwells be-side a blue stream's tide, That bounds thro' wild Glen-roe; Through ev'-ry change her love's the same, A long bright sum-mer dawn, A gen-tle flame, and O, her name, Is love-ly Mar-gred Bawn, O joy, that on her paths I came, My love-ly Mar-gred Bawn!

When winter hoar comes freezing o'er the mountains wild and gray,
Her neck is white as snow-wreaths bright, upon thy crags Knockea;
Her lips are red as roses sweet on Darra's flow'ry lawn:
Her fairy feet are light and fleet, my gentle Margred Bawn;
And O, her steps I love to meet, my own dear Margred Bawn!

When silence creeps o'er Houra's steeps, as blue eve ends her reign,
Her long locks' fold is like the gold that gleams o'er sky and main.
My heart's fond sorrow fled away like night before the dawn,
When one spring day, I went astray, and met my Margred Bawn,
And felt her blue eyes' sparkling ray, my lovely Margred Bawn.

One summer noon to hear the tune of wild birds in the wood,
Where murmuring streams flashed back the beams, all rapt in bliss I stood;
The birds sang from the fairy moat, from greenwood, brake, and lawn;
But never throat could chant a note so sweet as Margred Bawn,
As through the vales her wild songs float, my lovely Margred Bawn.

O, would that we for love could flee to some far valley green,
Where never more by rock or shore, dark sorrow could be seen.
I know a valley, wildly fair, from strife far, far withdrawn;
And ever there the loving air of gentle Margred Bawn,
Would keep this fond heart free from care, my lovely Margred Bawn.

No. 90.

I took down this beautiful air in Dublin, in the year 1854, from the singing of a servant named Mary Hackett, a native of the county Limerick.

PRETTY PEGGY.

♩ = pend. 30 inches.

Slowly and with expression.

No. 91.

THE BOYS OF THE TOWN. Jig.   ♩. = pend. 10 inches.

94   ANCIENT IRISH MUSIC.

No. 92.

This tune, which I think a very fine one, I noted down in Dublin, from the singing of a servant named Jane Murphy, a native of Laytown near Drogheda.

No. 93.

I have known the air and the words of this song as long as I can remember. The song contains six verses, one or two of which are good, but the rest are very poor.

Instead of the old song, I give the following one of my own, founded on it. The first verse is the same as it stands in the original, and the third is very little changed.

ADIEU LOVELY MARY.

"Adieu, lovely Mary, I'm now going to leave you, To the burning East Indies my sad voyage to steer; I know very well my long absence will grieve you; Sweetheart, I'll be back in the spring of the year."

"To the burning East Indies, I'll go love, along with you,
"Your bride I shall be, and no danger I'll fear;
"I'll dress myself up in the dress of a sailor;
"And I'll go with my love till the spring of the year."

3. "Your delicate fingers cold cables can't handle,
   "Your small pretty feet to the mast can't go near;
   "And your delicate body cold winds can't endure:
   "Be advised, love, and stay till the spring of the year."

4. "I care not for tempests while you, love, are by me;
   "I'll be safe on the billows if you, love, are near;
   "I fear not the cold nor the wild raging ocean;
   "And, sweetheart, we'll return in the spring of the year."

5. "O cease, lovely Mary, I'm not going to leave you;
   "I'll not leave you, dear Mary, in anguish and fear;
   "I have gold in my coffers, I've herds and broad pastures;
   "And my bride you shall be in the spring of the year."

No. 94.

From James Buckley, a Limerick piper.

STROP THE RAZOR. Jig.

No. 96.

There are few tunes better known all over Munster than this; and a number of songs are sung to it, of which I know portions of at least half-a-dozen. The following stanza of one will be sufficient to shew the measure and rhythm of all.

By the Blackwater side, not far from Castle-Hyde, there dwells a most beautiful creature;
She's slender tall and straight, and in beauty quite complete, and charming in every feature,
I met her the other day as I roved along the way, and I asked where my darling was going;
She said she meant to go as far as Templenoe, and I begged to accompany my storeen.

DOBBIN'S FLOWERY VALE.

No. 97.

I learned this fine old melody from my father: there is an Irish song to it, which is still current among the people of Cork and Limerick; but up to the time of sending this sheet to press I have not been able to procure a copy of it. This air must not be confounded with another very different melody, "Oonagh," to which Moore has written his song "While gazing on the moon's light." The two names are however the same, though spelled differently.

UNA.

Slow and with expression.

No. 98.

I took this sportive pretty air in 1853, from Joseph Martin, (see page 5); but I have since heard it sung in Dublin by Jane Murphy (p. 94), to a song of which this is the only part I can remember:—

"O, my darling girl I'll soon come back and surely marry you!"

As I cannot produce the old song, perhaps the following *jeu d'esprit* of my own will answer as well. As to the subject :—it may be necessary to state, for the information of those who are not acquainted with Irish fairies, that the leprehaun is a very tricky little fellow, usually dressed in a green coat, red cap and knee-breeches, and silver shoe-buckles, whom you may sometimes see in the shades of evening, or by moonlight, under a bush; and he is generally making or mending a shoe: moreover, like almost all fairies, he would give the world for *pottheen*. If you catch him and hold him, he will, after a little threatening, shew you where treasure is hid, or give you a purse in which you will always find money. But if you once take your eyes off him, he is gone in an instant; and he is very ingenious in devising tricks to induce you to look round.

It is very hard to catch a leprehaun, and still harder to hold him. I never heard of any man, who succeeded in getting treasure from him, except one, a lucky young fellow named MacCarthy, who according to the peasantry, built the castle of Carrigadrohid near Macroom in Cork, with the money.

Every Irishman understands well the terms *cruiskeen* and *mountain dew*, some indeed a little too well: but for the benefit of the rest of the world, I think it better to state that a *cruiskeen* is a small jar, and that *mountain dew* is *pottheen* or illicit whiskey.

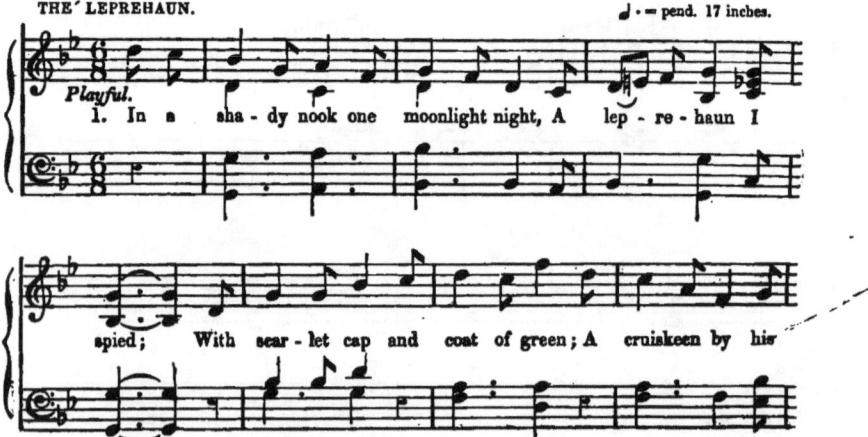

THE LEPREHAUN.

Playful.

1. In a sha-dy nook one moonlight night, A lep-re-haun I spied; With scar-let cap and coat of green; A cruiskeen by his

2. With tip-toe step and beating heart,
   Quite softly I drew nigh:
   There was mischief in his merry face;—
   A twinkle in his eye.
   He hammered and sang with tiny voice,
   And drank his mountain dew;
   And I laughed to think he was caught at last:—
   But the fairy was laughing too!

3. As quick as thought I seized the elf;
   "Your fairy purse!" I cried;
   "The purse!" he said—"'tis in her hand—
   "That lady at your side!"
   I turned to look: the elf was off!
   Then what was I to do?
   O, I laughed to think what a fool I'd been;
   And the fairy was laughing too!

No. 99.

Taken down from Lewis O'Brien, already spoken of at page 24.

ANCIENT IRISH MUSIC.   103

No. 100.

I took down this very characteristic air and one verse of the song, from Peggy Cudmore, already mentioned (page 16). In the month of September of the present year, I got two complete manuscript copies of the song; one from Kerry, and the other from Mayo; for it is well known in both the south and the west. It is obvious that the ballad relates a real event—the accidental drowning of poor young Willy Leonard. There are many places in Ireland called Coolfin; but in which of them "The Lake of Coolfin" is situated I cannot tell.

The ballad, as I received it (and the two versions do not differ materially), is a singular mixture of vigour and imbecility; in some parts vivid and true to nature; in others, vulgar, feeble and prosy. I have curtailed the tedious matter of fact narrative at the end, and retrenched other parts also; added something of my own; changed many of the lines; and restored the rhythm where it was necessary. But I have retained as much of the old ballad as possible.

THE LAKE OF COOLFIN; or WILLY LEONARD.   ♩ = pend. 24 inches.
Andante.

1. 'Twas ear-ly one morning young Wil-ly a-rose, And up to his comrade's bed-cham-ber he goes: "A-rise, my dear comrade, and let no one know; 'Tis a fine sun-ny morning and a bathing we'll go."

To the Lake of Coolfin the companions soon came,
And the first man they met was the keeper of game:—
"Turn back Willy Leonard, return back again;
"There is deep and false water in the Lake of Coolfin!"

Young Willy plunged in, and he swam the lake round;
He swam to an island—'twas soft marshy ground:
"O, comrade, dear comrade, do not venture in;
"There is deep and false water in the Lake of Coolfin!"

'Twas early that morning his sister arose;
And up to her mother's bed-chamber she goes:—
"O, I dreamed a sad dream about Willy last night;
"He was dressed in a shroud—in a shroud of snow-white!"

'Twas early that morning his mother came there;
She was wringing her hands—she was tearing her hair.
O, woful the hour your dear Willy plunged in:—
There is deep and false water in the Lake of Coolfin!

And I saw a fair maid, standing fast by the shore;
Her face it was pale—she was weeping full sore;
In deep anguish she gazed where young Willy plunged in:—
Ah! there's deep and false water in the Lake of Coolfin!

FINIS.

LIST OF SUBSCRIBERS.

ABBOTT, T. K., Esq., Fellow, Trinity College, Dublin.
Abraham, G. W., Esq., LL. D., Dublin.
Adair, John G., Esq., B. A., Monasterevin.
Adair, Samuel, Esq., A. M., Athy.
Adams, Charles Stuart, Esq., J. P., Newbliss.
Adams, William Henry, Esq., Dublin.
Alexander, Thomas, Esq., Dublin.
Allen, Capt. A. P., Dublin.
Allman, Rev. W., A. B., M. D., Carrigart.
Anketell, Rev. Thomas, Magheracloone.
Armstrong, Andrew, Esq., M. R. I. A., Dublin.
Armstrong, Rev. William B., A. M., Caledon.
Ashtown, Right Hon. Lord, Clonodfoy, Kilfinane.
Ashtown, Right Hon. Lady, do. do.
Askwith, William H., Esq., Liverpool.
Atkinson, Mrs. H., Frankville, Athboy.
Aylmer, Sir Gerald George, Bart., Donadea.

BAGOTT, John Lloyd, Esq., Durrow, Ballymoe.
Barry, James G., Esq., J. P., Sandville, Kilmallock.
Barton, Rev. Luke, P. P., Castletown-G.
Bayley, R. P., Esq., D. L., Rookwood, Athleague.
Beamish, Thomas, Esq., Jun., J. P., Timoleague.
Beatty, Rev. J., A. M., Killaghtee.
Beauchamp, R. H., Esq., J. P., Kildare-street Club, Dublin.
Bell, Hamilton, Esq., Dublin.
Bellew, Miss, Dublin.
Bernard, Hon. Mrs., Tuam Palace, Galway.
Birnie, Thomas M., Esq., J. P., Carrickfergus.
Blacker, Rev. Beaver H., A. M., Blackrock, Dublin.
Bloomfield, Right Hon. Lord, Moneygall.
Blundell, Rev. Robert, A. M., Headford.
Bodkin, Mrs., Ballyglunin, Galway.
Booth, Sir Robert Gore, Bart., Lissadill.
Bossonet, Julius, Esq., B. Sc., U. F., Dublin.
Bourke, Rev. Ulick J., Canon, St. Jarlath's, Tuam.
Boyle, Hugh, Esq., J. P., Armagh.
Brady, Rev. Francis T., A. M., Clonmel.
Brady, Sir Francis W., Bart., Dublin.
Brash, Richard R., Esq., Cork.
Brennan, George, Esq., Clifden.
Brett, —— Esq., Belfast.
Brooke, Thomas, Esq., D. L., Lough Eske, Donegal.
Brown, William, Esq., Dublin.
Browne, James, Esq., Donoughmore, Tyrone.
Brogan, Michael, Esq., Dublin.
Buckmaster, William, Esq., M. D., Midleton.

Burgess, J. Tom, Esq., Leamington.
Burke, G. E., Esq., J. P., Danesfield, Moycullen.
Burke, Sir J. Bernard, Ulster King at Arms, Dublin.
Burton, Miss, Dublin.
Butler, Edward, Esq., A. M., Dublin.
Butler, Most Rev. George, D. D., Bishop of Limerick.
Byrne, James, Esq., Wallstown, Shanballymore.
Byrne, Henry, Esq., Dublin.
Byrne, Miss, Dublin.
Byrne, Rev. Laurence, Adm., Portadown.

CAHILL, James, Esq., Dublin.
Campbell, Robert, Esq., A. M., Dublin.
Carey, Rev. P., P. P., Borris, Carlow.
Carroll, D. W., Esq., Dublin.
Casement, Julius, Esq., A. M., J. P., Cronroe, Ashford.
Casement, Thomas, Esq., J. P., Ballee, Ballymena.
Cather, Thos., Esq., A. B., J. P., Newtownlimavady.
Chamney, Rev. Joseph, Dromiskin.
Chamney, R. M., Esq., Dublin.
Cheevers, Michael J., Esq., Killyan, Ballinasloe.
Churchill, William, Esq., Belfast.
Claridge, James, Esq., Ed. Office, Dublin.
Clarke, James, Esq., Dublin.
Clermont, Lady, Ravensdale Park, Newry.
Close, Rev. Maxwell H., Blackrock, Dublin.
Cogan, Right Hon. W. H. F., M. P., Tinode, Co. Wicklow.
Colgan, Francis, Esq., J. P., Cappagh, Enfield.
Colquhoun, Sir James, Bart., Rossdhu, Luss, Scotland.
Commins, Rev. James, P. P., Castlegar, Galway.
Connellan, Peter, Esq., Roscommon.
Connolly, Robert E., Esq., Haddington.
Conran, Rev. J., P. P., Manaloy, Summerhill.
Considine, H., Esq., Derk, Pallasgrean.
Conway, John, Esq., Dublin.
Conwell, Eugene, Esq., LL. D., M. R. I. A., Trim.
Cope, Sir William, Bart., Hartfordbridge, Hampshire.
Corbett, John, Esq., A. M., Dublin.
Corry, Michael, Esq., Ballyconnell.
Cosgrave, Rev. M., P. P., Oylegate.
Costello, Rev. Bartholomew, P. P., Crosmolina.
Costello, J. J., Esq., Dublin.
Coyle, Michael, Esq., Portarlington.
Craig, Rev. George, A. M., Aghanloo, Magilligan.
Craig, Rev. J. Duncan, Kingstown, Dublin.

LIST OF SUBSCRIBERS.

Cree, George, Esq., Barrister, Dublin.
Cronin, Bartholomew, Kilcorney, Banteer.
Cruise, F. R., Esq., M. D., Dublin.
Cruise, Robert R., Esq., J. P., Drynan, Malahide.
Cullen, Carncross Thos., Esq., D. L., J. P., Glenade, Manorhamilton.
Currey, F. E., Esq., J. P., Lismore Castle.

DALTON, Richard, Esq., Tipperary.
Dames, Captain T. Longworth, D. L., Edenderry.
Davis, Mrs., Kenilworth-square, Dublin.
Davis, Thomas Perrin, J. P., Dalkey.
Day, John Fitzgerald, Esq., J. P., Killarney.
Dease, James Arthur, Esq., J. P., Turbotstown.
Delany, Rev. James J., Templetuohy.
Dell, Mr., Belfast.
De Vere, Aubrey, Esq., Curragh Chase, Adare.
De Vere, Stephen E., Esq., J. P., Foynes.
Devine, Mrs., Dublin.
Disney, Rev. James, Killyman, Moy.
Dixon, Rev. Robert V., D. D., Clogherny.
Dobbin, Rev. O. T., LL. D., Ballivor, Kells.
Donnelly, Rev. Nicholas, C. C., Dublin.
Donovan, James T., P. P., Parsonstown, Slane.
Donovan, Morgan, Esq., Dublin.
Doran, James, Randalstown.
Doran, Mr. George, Belfast.
Doran, Henry, Esq., Killarney.
Dowling, F., Esq., Waterford.
Dowling, Joseph, Esq., Dublin.
Downing, Denis P., Esq., Dublin.
Downing, Rev. W. F., Lyme Regis.
Downes, Rev. Thomas, D. D., Kilmallock.
Drislane, Mr. William, Tarbert.
Dudgeon, The Rev. Walter, V. G., Castlewellan.
Dugan, C. W., Esq., A. M., Parsonstown.
Duggan, Michael, Esq., Dublin.
Dunboyne, Right Hon. Lord, Knoppogue Castle.
Dunlop, R. T., Esq., Monasterboice.
Dunne, George, Esq., Dublin.
Dunne, John W., Esq., J. P., Stradbally, Queen's County.
Durham, Miss, Dublin.
Dwane, Thomas M., Esq., L. R. C. S. I., Cloyne.
Dyas, N. Hone, Esq., J. P., Athboy.

EAGAR, E. M'G., Esq., J. P., Killorglin, Kerry.
Edwards, Rev. William, A. M., Strabane.
Egan, Richard, Esq., M. D., Talbot-street, Dublin.
Esmonde, Sir John, Bart., D. L., J. P., Ballynastragh, Gorey.
Esmonde, Lady, Ballynastragh, Gorey.

FALLS, Thomas, Esq., Dublin.
Farlow, Samuel, Esq., Dublin.
Falconer, John, Esq., Dublin.
Fegen, Fredk. James, R. N., J. P., Ballinlonty, Borrisoleigh.
Fennelly, R., Esq., M. D., Glasnevin, Dublin.
Fennelly, Rev. John, P. P., Annacarty, Tipperary.
Ferguson, Joseph, Esq., M. D., Mullingar.
Ferguson, Samuel, Esq., LL. D., Q. C., Dublin.
Fitzgerald, J. G., Esq., A. B., Enniscorthy.
Fitzgerald, Rev. John, P. P., Kiltoom.
Fitzgerald, Right Hon. Judge, Dublin.
Fitzgerald, Michael, Esq., Dublin.
Fitzgerald, Peter, Esq., Knight of Kerry.

Fitzgibbon, Gerald, Esq., Jun., Q. C., Dublin.
Fitzpatrick, Rev. Fredk. A. M., Cloon, Mohill.
Fleming, Mr. John, Portlaw.
Fleming, Mr. John, Rathcormack.
Fleming, Miss, Rush, Dublin.
Fleming, Mr. Peter, Killarney.
Flood, Mr. P. W., Tullycrine, Kilrush.
Foley, Rev. W., C. C.
Fortescue, Right Hon. C. P., M. P., London.
Freeman, Rev. Francis E., Dungannon.
Frost, James, Esq., J. P., Ballymorris, Cratloe.

GAFFNEY, Rev. James, C. C., Coolock, Dublin.
Gage, Rev. Robert, A. B., Coleraine.
Galbraith, John S., Esq., J. P., Clonabogan.
Gallagher, Mr. Jeremiah, Dublin.
Galwey, Richard P., Esq., Cork.
Garnett, William, Esq., J. P., Castlerea.
Garstin, J. Ribton, Esq., LL. B., F. S. A., Dublin.
Garvey, Capt. Geo., R. N., J. P., Moneygall.
Gaskin, J. J., Esq., Belfast.
Geoghegan, Jacob W., Esq., Dublin.
Geoghegan, Rev. Thos., P. P., Boycetown.
Gibbons, J. H., Esq., Dublin.
Giblert, J. T., Esq., F. R. S., Dublin.
Gibson, James, Esq., Q. C., Mountjoy-square, Dublin.
Gibson, J. Westby, Esq., LL. D., Limerick.
Gillman, Major Bennett W., Clonakilty.
Goodman, Mr. Thomas, Belfast.
Goodman, Rev. James, Skibbereen.
Gordon, J., Esq., Newtownardes.
Granard, Right Hon. Lord, Castle-Forbes.
Graves, Rev. James, Inisnag, Kilkenny.
Greene, James, Esq., Glanworth, Fermoy.
Greene, Rev. William C., A. M., Dublin.
Greville, Miss, Dublin.
Grogan, Rev. Charles James, Dunleckny, Bagnalstown.
Guarini, Mrs., Dublin.
Gumbleton, Wm. E., Esq., J. P., Queenstown.
Gun, H. Murray, Esq., J. P., Newcastle West.
Gunn, Michael, Esq., Grafton-street, Dublin.

HALL, Henry, Esq., Herman-Villa, Woolston.
Hall, Thomas, Esq., Dublin.
Hallinan, Timothy, Esq., Deebert, Kilmallock.
Halpin, Rev. John, P. P., Kilfinane.
Hamilton, Mrs., Desertmartin, Magherafelt.
Hanlon, Rev. A. P., Ballyhamlet, Tallow.
Hanlon, John, Esq., Carlow.
Hannon, J., Esq., Cahir.
Harkin, Alexander, Esq., M. D., Belfast.
Harkin, Lewis, Esq., Kilkenny.
Hare, Ven. Charles, Archdeacon, Limerick.
Harpur, James, Esq., J. P., Drogheda.
Harpur, Rev. Thos. B., Frankford, King's Co.
Harpur, Rev. S. C., A. M., Aghaboe.
Harte, Miss, Cahir.
Hartnett, Mr. John, Lyre, Banteer.
Harvey, Edmund, Esq., Grange, Waterford.
Hastings, Right Hon. Lord, Sharavogue, Roscrea.
Headly, Right Hon. Lord, Aghadoe, Killarney.
Hennessy, Rev. M., C. C., Meelin, Newmarket.
Hennessy, Richard, Esq., Dublin.
Hennessy, W. M., Esq., M. R. I. A., Dublin.
Henry, Mitchell, Esq., M. P., Kylemore, Galway.

LIST OF SUBSCRIBERS.

Hickson, Robert C., Esq., J. P., Castlegregory.
Hogan, Rev. James W., Magherafelt.
Hogan, Mrs., Dublin.
Horan, William, Esq., Dublin.
Horan, Thomas, Esq., Dublin.
Horgan, Rev. John, P. P., Ballinspittle.
Hort, Sir John W., Bart., D. L., Dublin.
Hughes, Rev. James, Administrator, Portadown.
Hull, Major Madden, J. P., Narrow-Water.
Hunt, Miss, Enniscorthy.
Hunte, Rev. Francis Le, Dublin.
Hunter, W. A., Esq., Ed. Office, Dublin.
Hurly, John, Esq., J. P., Fenit, Tralee.
Hutchinson, Wm. Ford, Esq., J. P., Ballymoney.
Hutton, Francis, Esq., Dublin.
Hutton, William, Esq., Dublin.

INGRAM, J. K., Esq., Fellow, Trin. Coll., Dublin.
Irvine, Mrs., Dromalane, Newry.

JELLETT, Rev. John H., S. F. T. C., Dublin.
Joly, H. C., Esq., Clonbologue, Kildare.
Joly, J. R., Esq., Dublin.
Jones, Thomas H., Esq., D. L, Moneyglass, Toomebridge.
Joy, Rev. J., P. P., Dunhill, Tramore.
Joynt, Wm. Lane, Esq., D. L., Dublin.

KANE, Mr. Thomas, Belfast.
Keenan, Patrick J., Esq., C. B., Resident Commissioner of Education, Dublin.
Kelly, Charles, Esq., Q. C., Dublin.
Kelly, D., Esq., Enniscorthy.
Kelly, Denis H., Esq., J. P., Dublin.
Kelly, Luke, Esq., Dublin.
Kelly, Most Rev. Francis, D. D., Bishop of Derry.
Kenealy, William, Esq., Mayor of Kilkenny.
Kenefick, Rev. Maurice, P. P., Rathcormack.
Kennedy, B. E., Esq., Ballylooby, Cahir.
Kennedy, Right Hon. T. F., Maybole, Scotland.
Kenney, J. C. Fitzgerald, J.P., M. R. I. A., Dublin.
Keon, Rev. William, C. C., Dublin.
Ker, A. Murray, Esq., D. L., Newbliss.
Kidd, Lewis, Esq., Belfast.
Kieran, Rev. Thomas, P. P., Swords.
Kildare, The Most Hon. the Marquess of, Carton, Maynooth.
Kingston, Right Hon. the Earl of, Kilronan Castle, Roscommon.
Kingstone, Alex. C., Esq., J.P., Mosstown, Longfd.
Kirchhoffer, Richard B., Esq., Ballyvourney.
Kirkpatrick, Mr. Francis, Dunmanway.
Kirwan, Miss, Castlebacket, Galway.
Knox, Vesey E., Esq., J. P., Shimnah, Co. Down.
Kyle, Rev. Samuel Moore, LL. D., Archdeacon of Cork.

LABAT, Rev. Edward, Roxboro', Killybegs.
Lahiffe, Mrs. D., Rathgar, Dublin.
Lake, Col. Henry Attwell, C. B., Dublin.
Leahy, His Grace, The Most Rev. Patrick, D. D., Archbishop of Cashel.
Leet, The Rev. Edward S., Dalkey.
Leitrim, Right Hon. The Earl of, Lough Rynn, Dromod.

Lemass, Peter, Esq., Dublin.
Leniban, P., Esq., Monaghan.
Lentaigne, John, Esq., M. D., D. L., Dublin.
L'Estrange, Thomas, Esq., Belfast.
Levey, R. M., Esq., Dublin.
Lewen, F. T., Esq., J. P., Cloghans, Tuam.
Lidwill, Captain Geo. J.P., Junior United Service, Club, London.
Lindsay, Miss, Dublin.
Listowel, Right Hon. The Earl of, Convamore, Mallow.
Lombard, J. F., Esq., J.P., South-hill, Rathmines.
Long, P. W., Esq., M. D., Dublin.
Loughnan, J. M., Esq., Ennis.
Lowry, Mr. John, Moville.
Lyle, Major H. C., R. A., Woolwich Common, S. E.
Lynch, Mr. John, Cahir.
Lynch, Mrs. Richard M., Phillimore Gardens, London.
Lynch, P. M., Esq., Dublin.
Lynch, Rev. D., C. C., Midleton.
Lyons, Robert D., Esq., F. R. C. P. I., Merrion-square, Dublin.
Lyons, William H., Esq., Croom Castle, Limerick.

MACAULAY, Miss, Redhall, Belfast.
Macaulay, P. T., Esq., Letterkenny.
Macartney, George T., Esq., J.P., Avonmore, Dublin.
Mac Cann, Rev. Hugh, P. P., Rasbarkin.
Mac Carthy, the Rev. C. F., D. D., Dublin.
Mac Carthy, James J., Esq., Architect, Dublin.
Mac Carthy, J., Esq., Dublin.
Mac Carthy, Miss, Dublin.
Mac Clintock, Charles E., Esq., Glendaragh, Lurgan.
Mac Creanor, Edward, Esq., Drogheda.
Mac Devitt, The Most Rev. James, Bishop of Raphoe.
Mac Donald, Wm., Esq., M. D., Killavullen, Cork.
Macdonnell, Rev. M. J., Canon, P. P., V. G., Listowel.
Macdonnell, J., Esq., Bantry.
Macdonnell, Right Hon. Sir Alexander, Bart., Dublin.
Macdonnell, Robert, Esq., M. D., F.R.S., Dublin.
Macdonnell, Mr. Patrick, Rathkeale.
Macdonnell, Lieut.-Col. W. E. A., Ennis.
Mac Eneany, P., Esq., Athy.
Mac Farlane, H. J., Esq., J. P., Huntstown, Mulhuddart.
Mac Gettigan, His Grace, The Most Rev. Daniel, Archbishop of Armagh.
Mac Hale, His Grace, The Most Rev. John, Archbishop of Tuam.
Mac Intosh, Rev. J. S., Belfast.
Mac Knight, James, Esq., LL. D., Derry.
Mac Laughlin, Rev. Thomas, LL. D., Viewforth, Edinburgh.
Mac Loughlin, Mr. P., Dromcollogher.
Mac Mahon, Rev. John, P. P., Mountnorris.
Mac Padden, Mr. Bartholomew, Dublin.
Mac Sheehy, Brian, Esq., LL. D., Ballybrack, Dublin.
Madden, H. J., Esq., M. D., Ballycastle, Mayo.
Madden, M. J., Esq., J. P., Camphill, Collooney.

LIST OF SUBSCRIBERS.

Maginn, Rev. Thos., P. P., Rosbeigh, Kerry.
Maguire, Rev. John M., A. M., Vermont, Clarina.
Mahaffy, Gilbert, Esq., A. M., Dublin.
Mahaffy, Rev. John P., Fellow, Trinity College, Dublin.
Malahide, Right Hon. Lord Talbot de, Malahide Castle.
Mansfield, George, Esq, Jun., J. P., Morristown, Naas.
Marlay, C. Brinsley, Esq., D. L., J. P., Regent's Park, London.
Martin, John, Esq., M. P., Warrenpoint.
Martin, Rev. John W., Timoleague.
Maunsell, Rev. W. F., Kildimo, Limerick.
Maunsell, Daniel Meares, Esq., J. P., Rathkeale.
M'Connell, Henry, Esq., Belfast.
M'Coy, Mr. William John, Belfast.
M'Grath, Mr. James, Belfast.
Meehan, Mr. Gilbert, Moate.
Minnett, J. R., Esq., J. P., Annabeg, Nenagh.
Molloy, John, Esq., Galway.
Molyneux, Ecblin, Esq., Q C., Bray.
Mooney, Rev. Daniel, P. P., Dungiven.
Moore, C. H., Esq., Dublin.
Moore, Robert L., Esq., J. P., Molenan, Derry.
Moore, William F., Esq., Dublin.
Moriarty, The Most Rev. Dr., Bishop of Kerry.
Morrin, Mr. John, Dublin.
Morris, Charles, Esq., Enniskillen.
Morrissey, Rev. A., C. C., Banteer, Cork.
Moutray, Henry, Esq., J. P., Aughnacloy.
Mulgan, Rev. William Mason, LL. D., Lisnadill.
Mulholland, John, Esq., D. L., J. P., Grey-Abbey.
Murphy, Edmund, Esq., J. P., Dunfanaghy.
Murphy, Miss, Dublin.

NEDLEY, Thomas, Esq., M. D., Rutland-square, Dublin.
Newell, W. H., Esq., LL. D., Gt. Charles-st., Dublin.
Newell, W. O'B., Esq., C. E., A. M.,   do.
Nicholls, William, Esq., Gort.
Nicholson, J. A., Esq., M. A., D. L., Balrath, Kells.
Norreys, Sir Denham, Bart., The Castle, Mallow.
North, James H., Esq., Dublin.

OAKES, William, Esq., Tyrrell's Pass.
O'Brien, Daniel, Esq., Kilgobinet.
O'Brien, Edward William, Esq., D. L., J. P., Cahirmoyle, Limerick.
O'Brien, Mr. Matthew, Belfast.
O'Brien, Mrs. John, Loughgur, Limerick.
O'Brien, Rev. Lucius H., A. M., Claragh, Ramelton.
O'Byrne, William, Esq., Dublin.
O'Connell, Rev. Cornelius, P. P., Meelin, Cork.
O'Connell, Morgan D., Esq., Kt. St. F., M. D., F. R. C. S. I., Kilmallock.
O'Connor, Matthew Weld, Esq., A. M., J. P., Viewmount, Longford.
O'Conor, Mrs., Dundermott, Ballymoe.
O'Doherty, Rev. J. K., Adm., Newtownstewart.
O'Doherty, Rev. William, Adm., Moville.
O'Donnell, Michael, Esq., Hill Cottage, Kilmallock.
O'Dowd, William, Esq., Dublin.
O'Donoghoe, Rev. Denis, P. P., Ardfert.
O'Duffy, John, Esq., Westland-row, Dublin.
O'Farrell, Michael R., Esq., J. P., Midleton.

O'Flaherty, George F., Esq., J. P., Lemonfield, Galway.
O'Gorman, Purcell, Esq., J. P., Springfield, Waterford.
O'Hagan, The Right Hon. Lord, Lord Chancellor.
O'Hara, Thomas, Esq., A. B., Clonmel.
O'Hare, Mr. James, Ligoniel, Belfast.
O'Keeffe, Rev. D., C. C., Dublin.
O'Kennedy, Rev. Daniel, P. P., Limerick.
O'Leary, Rev. Edmund, P. P., Toomavara.
O'Leary, Miss, Dublin.
O'Longan, Joseph, Esq., R. I. A., Dublin.
O'Looney, Brian, Esq., Dublin.
O'Mahony, The Rev. Thaddeus, D.D., Feighcullen.
O'Mulrenin, Richard J., Esq., Dublin.
O'Neill, Hon. Robert, Shane's Castle, Antrim.
O'Regan, Ven. P. D., P. P., Archdeacon of Cloyne.
O'Regan, Ven. John. Archdeacon of Kildare.
O'Reilly, Mr. Michael, Grange, Bruff.
O'Reilly, Michael, Esq., Clonmel.
O'Rourke, Rev. T., D D., P. P., Collooney.
Orpen, Mrs., Killaha Castle, Killarney.
Orpen, Rev. Raymond d'A., A. M., Tralee.
Orpen, Richard A., Esq., J. P., Elm Park, Cork.
Osborne, A. T., Esq., Armagh.
O'Shanahan, James, Esq., Dublin.
O'Shanessy, Francis, Esq., Athy.
O'Shea, Rev. James, P. P., V. G., Rathkeale.
O'Sullivan, Daniel, Esq., Ph. D., M. R. I. A., Dublin.
O'Sullivan, John, Esq., Bruff.
O'Sullivan, Rev. G., P. P., Parteen, Limerick.
O'Sullivan, Rev. John, P. P., V. G., Kenmare.
O'Sullivan, William H., Esq., Kilmallock.
O'Sullivan, William, Esq., Jun.,   do.

PALMER, Charles C., Esq., J. P., Rahan, Edenderry.
Paterson, Major, Clifden House, Corrofin, Clare.
Pemberton, Miss, Dublin.
Penny, Charles, Esq., Dublin.
Phillips, James, Esq., Durrus, Cork.
Porter, Miss, Belleisle, Lisbellaw, Fermanagh.
Porter, Rev. Thomas H., Ballymully, Tyrone.
Potterton, Robert, Esq., LL. D., Limerick.
Posnett, George, Esq., J. P., Bray.
Power, Rev. Richard, P. P., Glenroe, Kilfinane.
Pratt, Rev. John, A. M., Durrus, Bantry.
Prendergast, Rev. James, P. P., Tallow.
Purdon, Charles D., Esq., M. B., F. R. C. S. I., Belfast.

QUIGLEY, Miss, Carysfort-Avenue, Blackrock.
Quin, Hugh, Esq., J. P., Creggan, Cookstown.
Quinn, Rev. Richard, P. P., Rusmuck, Galway.
Quirk, Ven. W., Archdeacon of Cashel.

RAE, Edward, Esq., J. P., Keel, Castlemaine.
Ray, T. M., Esq., Jun., Dublin.
Reade, Philip, Esq., M. A., J. P., Scariff, Clare.
Reeves, Rev. William, D. D., LL. D., Tynan, Armagh.
Reid, Robert, Esq., Moate House, Hollywood.
Reide, Rev. George H., J. P., Inniskeen, Dundalk.
Rice, Rev. Thomas, C. C., Moy, Tyrone.
Rintoul, John, Esq., A. M., Dublin.
Robinson, Joseph, Esq., Dublin.

LIST OF SUBSCRIBERS.

Roberts, The Rev. S., A. B., Blackrock, Dublin.
Robertson, Charles, Esq., A. M., Dublin.
Roche, Rev. J. L., P. P., Banogue, Limerick.
Rodgers, John W., Esq., A. M., Belfast.
Roney, Mr. Thomas, Dublin.
Rowley, Standish G., Esq., J. P., M. R. I. A., Kells.
Rowan, Rev. Edward, C. C., Glendalough.
Ruddell, Mr. Thomas, Belfast.
Ryan, Arthur, Esq., Scarteen, Knocklong.
Ryan, Laurence, Esq., Kilkenny.
Ryan, Rev. Martin, P. P., Athea, Limerick.
Ryan, Patrick, Esq., Dublin.
Ryan, Mr. Patrick, Kilfinane.
Rynn, Mr. John, Dublin.

St. George, James, Esq., Oranmore, Galway.
Saunders, Michael, Esq., Portlaw.
Scott, Rev. J. George, Bray.
Scroope, Henry, Esq., J. P., Ballystanley, Roscrea.
Scully, Mr. John, Belfast.
Shaw, Rev. Robert, The Deanery, Armagh.
Shearman, Rev. J. F., C. C., Howth, Dublin.
Sheridan, John E., Esq., Ed. Office, Dublin.
Sheridan, Mr. Bernard, Bray.
Shields, Mr. Thomas, Belfast.
Shirley, Evelyn P., Esq., J. P., Carrickmacross.
Shirley, Thomas, Esq., Kilkenny.
Shuldham, Captain E. A., Coolkellure, Dunmanway.
Sigerson, George, Esq., M. D., Dublin.
Simes, N. P., Esq., J. P., Newport, Mayo.
Sinclair, Mrs., Bonnyglen, Inver, Donegal.
Smart, Mr. John, Glenalla, Letterkenny.
Smith, George H., Esq., Limerick.
Smith, William, Esq., Dublin.
Smyth, Hon. Mrs. More, Ballynatray, Youghal.
Smythe, Major-General J., Coole, Carnmoney.
Smythe, W. B., Esq., D. L., J. P., Barbavilla, Killucan.
Somerville, Thomas, Esq., D. L., J. P., Drishane, Skibbereen.
Spillane, Mr. Maurice, Farrahy, Co. Cork.
Sproule, Thomas, Esq., J. P., Altnamullen, Strabane.
Stack, Denis, Esq., Castle Hyde, Fermoy.
Stack, Rev. Charles M., A. M., Kilmarran, Monaghan.
Stawell, Col. W. St. Leger Alcock, Kilbrittain, Bandon.
Stawell, Mrs. Alcock, Do. Do.
Steede, John, Esq., Newcastle West.
Stevenson, Robert, Esq., Dublin.
Stevenson, Rev. W. Fleming, Rathgar.
Stewart, Augusta L., the Viscountess, Oaklands, Cookstown.
Stewart, James R., Esq., J. P., Dublin.
Stewart, Thomas Blakeny Lyon, Esq., J. P., Midleton.
Stokes, Miss, Merrion-square, Dublin.
Stritch, Thomas, Esq., Dublin.
Stuart, Ven. Alexander, A. M., Archd. of Ross.
Style, Hon. Mrs., Brecon, South Wales.
Sullivan, Daniel, Esq., Dublin.
Sullivan, William K., Esq., Ph. D., Dublin.

Swift, Rev. Travers, A. M., Kilbixy, Ballynacargy.
Synge, Rev. Edward, Mus. Doc., Parsonstown.
Taaffe, Rev. George, P. P., Collon, Drogheda.
Talbot, John, Esq., Aghadoe, Killarney.
Tardy, Rev. Elias, A. B., J. P., Ballybay.
Taylor, Joseph P., Esq., Dublin.
Thom, Alexander W., Esq., J. P., Donnycarney, Dublin.
Thompson, Hamlet, Esq., J. P., Banagher.
Thompson, H. Y., Esq., Private Secretary's Lodge, Dublin.
Thompson, Millar, Esq., Dublin.
Tighe, Right Hon. Colonel, Woodstock, Inistioge.
Tighe, Lady Elizabeth, do. do.
Tighe, James, Esq., Dublin.
Todd, Arthur, Esq., Ed. Office, Dublin.
Toal, Henry, Esq., Moy, Tyrone.
Toleken, John, Esq., M. D., S. F. T. C., Dublin.
Tottenham, Rev. Henry, B. D., Fintona, Tyrone.
Towers, P., Esq., Capel-street, Dublin.
Townsend, Mrs., Louth, Dundalk.
Townsend, Rev. William C., Castlebar.
Trant, John, Esq., D. L., J. P., Dovea, Thurles.
Trench, J. Townsend, Esq., J. P., Kenmare.
Tuomy, Rev. John, P. P., Dromtarriffe, Dromagh.
Tyrrell, Ward, Esq., Haddington-road, Dublin.

Uniacke, Miss, Ballyee, Cork.
Upton, Major A. S., Coolatoor, Moate.

Waldron, Laurence, Esq., D. L., J. P., Rutland-square, Dublin.
Wall, John, Esq., Dublin.
Wall, R. N., Esq., J. P., Glear, Clones.
Walsh, Rev. John, P. P., Aughaviller, Knocktopher.
Walsh, Rev. Edmund, P. P., Rathmore.
Walsh, J. R., Esq., Martinstown, Kilmallock.
Walsh, Stephen H., Esq., Kilmallock.
Ward, Robert E., Esq., J. P., Bangor, Belfast.
Warner, Rev. Gustavus, A.M., Castlelost, Killucan.
Waters, Thomas G., Esq., Kilpatrick, Monasterovan.
Watson, Rev. J. M., A. M., Leighlinbridge.
Watson, William James, Esq., C. E., Newry.
Webb, Alfred, Esq., Dublin.
Webster, Rev. George, D. D., Cork.
Whelan, Rev. R. W., The Rectory, Maynooth.
White, Rev. George P., The Rectory, Golden.
Wilde, Sir William R., Merrion-square, Dublin.
Wilde, Rev. Ralph, Hollymount, Down.
Williams, William, Esq., Dungarvan.
Wilson, Charles M., Esq., F. R. S., Limerick.
Wilson, Mrs., Laghey, Donegal.
Wilson, Rev. Hugh, LL. B., Ballywalter, Down.
Wren, Edmund, Esq., M. A., Belfast.
Wrenn, Rev. George, M. A., Kilfinane.
Wrey, Mrs., Lyme Regis.
Wynne, Captain Owen, D. L., J. P., Hazlewood.

Young, G. A., Esq., Dublin.
Young, George, Esq., D. L., J. P., Culdaff, Donegal.
Young, Rev. Walter, A. M., Templecarn, Donegal.

www.ingramcontent.com/pod-product-compliance
Lightning Source LLC
Chambersburg PA
CBHW031354160426
43196CB00007B/814